A VERY BRIEF INTRODUCTION TO REFORMATION DOCTRINE

A Very Brief Introduction to Reformation Doctrine

CORNELIU C. SIMUȚ

CASCADE *Books* • Eugene, Oregon

A VERY BRIEF INTRODUCTION TO REFORMED DOCTRINE

Copyright © 2024 Corneliu C. Simuț. All rights reserved. Except for brief quotations in critical publications or reviews, no part of this book may be reproduced in any manner without prior written permission from the publisher. Write: Permissions, Wipf and Stock Publishers, 199 W. 8th Ave., Suite 3, Eugene, OR 97401.

Cascade Books
An Imprint of Wipf and Stock Publishers

199 W. 8th Ave., Suite 3
Eugene, OR 97401
www.wipfandstock.com

PAPERBACK ISBN: 978-8-3852-0054-2
HARDCOVER ISBN: 978-8-3852-0055-9
EBOOK ISBN: 978-8-3852-0056-6

Cataloguing-in-Publication data:

Names: Simuț, Corneliu C., author.

Title: A very brief introduction to Reformed doctrine / Corneliu C. Simuț.

Description: Eugene, OR: Cascade Books, 2024. | Includes bibliographical references and indexes.

Identifiers: ISBN 978-8-3852-0054-2 (paperback). | ISBN 978-8-3852-0055-9 (hardcover). | ISBN 978-8-3852-0056-6 (epub).

Subjects: LSCH: Reformation—Theology. | Theology, Doctrinal—History—16th century. | Theology, Doctrinal—Lutheran. | Theology, Doctrinal—Reformed. | Theology, Doctrinal—Anabaptist. | Theology, Doctrinal—Roman Catholic.

Classification: BR305.3 S56 2024 (print). | BR305.3 (epub).

to my son, Ezra,
as he sets sail to study theology

Contents

Preface | ix

1 Introduction: Methodologies and Theologians | 1
2 Humanist Theology: Jacques Lefèvre d'Etaples and Desiderius Erasmus of Rotterdam | 11
3 Lutheran Theology (1): Martin Luther and Philip Melanchthon | 21
4 Lutheran Theology (2): Matthias Flacius and Argula von Grumbach | 31
5 Lutheran Theology (3): Urbanus Rhegius, Johannes Brenz, and Martin Chemnitz | 40
6 Reformed Theology (1): Ulrich Zwingli and Heinrich Bullinger | 50
7 Reformed Theology (2): Jean Calvin and Pietro Martire Vermigli | 60
8 Reformed Theology (3): Théodore de Bèze, Katharina Schütz Zell, and Martin Bucer | 69
9 Reformed Theology (4): Thomas Cranmer and Richard Hooker | 78
10 Catholic Theology (1): Tomasso de Vio Cajetan and Thomas More | 87

11 Catholic Theology (2): Ignatius of Loyola
    and Theresa d'Ávila | 96

12 Radical Theology (1): Andreas Bodenstein von Karlstadt
    and Thomas Müntzer | 104

13 Radical Theology (2): Caspar Schwenckfeld
    and Menno Simons | 113

14 Conclusion: The Impact of Reformation Theology | 123

Bibliography | 131

Preface

THIS BOOK IS A very short course in the history of Christian dogma, which serves as an introduction to Reformation doctrine. While light years away from an exhaustive study in the complexity of Reformation thought, history, and philosophy, this fourteen-lesson based brief introduction is merely an attempt to help students get a decent grasp of the Reformation's most basic precepts. Consequently, it eludes the vastity of Reformation dogmatic sophistication by focusing primarily on the doctrine of justification, the very reason why the Reformation not only began as a dogmatic effort to renew the church but also successfully made it as an ecclesiastical movement with countless cultural effects throughout the world.

It should be stressed from the onset that this is not a material for established scholars, researchers or even teachers of the Reformation. It is not meant to help professionals in the field of Reformation studies or even trained theologians who want to clarify various aspects of the Reformation, regardless of whether they be dogmatic or otherwise. This little course is for students and especially people who never heard of the Reformation; for those who wish to acquire a swift perspective on the most fundamental facets of Reformation theology—it is for beginners and people whose time is so scarce that they can hardly pick up anything to read. But if or when they do decide to read something in the field of Reformation studies, and if they do come across this brief introduction, then a light reading across no more than merely a fortnight should be enough for them to understand the basics of Reformation thinking.

The course is built on scattered notes that I piled up throughout my twenty-five-year-long career in teaching theology at various levels, but this one is meant to help bachelor students and lay people whose interest in the Reformation as a dominantly religious phenomenon is strong enough to prompt them to read something about it. Historical elements are scarce and

Preface

cultural insights almost non-existent; this is why the course aims to provide information about Reformation doctrine, about the teaching of the most basic elements of Reformation dogma. In the end, this whole effort—brief and insignificant as it is—was designed to assist those who are new to the subject of Reformation theology to acquire at least the basic theological language and concepts required to help them become confident in their future investigations into the universe of Reformation thought.

Although focused on doctrine and theology, this very concise introduction is written from the perspective of a dogma historian. No sides are taken in any way; Protestants and Catholics are treated evenly from the perspective of their contribution to the Reformation of the church in the sixteenth century—thus, for the purposes of this study, Protestants and Catholics alike are equally important. The number of Protestant theologians vastly outruns that of their Catholic counterparts; the Reformation is, after all, a predominantly Protestant phenomenon. Nevertheless, what the Catholic Church also did through its representatives during the long sixteenth century to enact genuine measures of ecclesiastical reform is taken into account and brought to the fore in two chapters dedicated to Catholic theologians whose lives were invested in making sure the church was renewed as earnestly and efficiently as possible.

It stands to reason that this small contribution to the hugely encompassing domain of Reformation research is far from competing with artful studies which investigate Protestant and Catholic sources from complex angles and variegated perspectives. Even so, undergraduate students and people who just want to know something about the teachings of the Reformation across its Protestant and Catholic representatives may find it not only easy to read but also enjoyable and useful.

Corneliu C. Simuț
Oradea, January 23, 2023

1

Introduction

Methodologies and Theologians

OBJECTIVES

1. To know the definition of the Reformation as a movement that includes Protestantism and Catholicism;
2. To become familiar with the various types of Reformation theology;
3. To grow aware of a range of methodologies which aim at the study and the interpretation of Reformation theology;
4. To identify the essence of Reformation theology with reference to the doctrine of justification by faith alone;
5. To be able to present the fundamental preoccupations of Reformation theology.

Key words: Reformation, Protestantism, Catholicism, humanism, history, theology

METHODOLOGIES CONCERNING THE STUDY OF REFORMATION THEOLOGY

Reformation theology does not refer exclusively to Protestantism but also to Catholicism; thus, this course presents the theology of some of the

A Very Brief Introduction to Reformation Doctrine

most famous Protestant and Catholic divines. Carter Lindberg[1] discloses that they were generally professors of theology, individuals with tertiary theological education, members of the clergy, lay people, men and women, but they were all promoters of the religious reformations of the sixteenth century both within the Catholic Church of Rome and the new Evangelical churches later known as Protestant, the most important of which were the Lutherans, the Reformed, and the Anabaptists. This is why Heinz Schilling believes that everything started with Luther, Loyola, and Calvin who were all strongly influenced by Jacques Lefèvre and Desiderius Erasmus, two of the best-known predecessors of the religious Reformations that spread across Europe back in those days.[2]

Why should we be interested in the study of the Reformation? First, because of the spiritual and intellectual ties which exist between the sixteenth-century Reformation and contemporary forms of Protestantism. Josef Korbel points out that the Reformation, which is a Western phenomenon, found "receptive soil" in Central and Eastern Europe[3] and, evidently, across the entire world. Second, we must be aware that Christian life, the church, and contemporary theology are built on the foundation provided by Reformation theology and its christological focus. In this respect, Andrew Murray writes that "justification by faith in Jesus Christ" was "the foundation of the Christian life" during the "Reformation period."[4] Third, we cannot be fully aware of our own theology without having some knowledge of Reformation theology. As Hans Schwarz put it, we must be aware of the "connection between our modern mindset"[5] and the early Christian tradition, including the Reformation. Fourth, it is compulsory to learn of the relationship we, as contemporary people, share with Reformation theology and its Catholic sources which, evidently, preceded the Reformation. Regardless of whether we acknowledge or reject Catholic sources, as shown by Duane Garrett,[6] Reformation theology is inextricably connected with Catholicism not only historically and theologically, but also intellectually and culturally.

---

1. Lindberg, "Introduction," 1.
2. Schilling, "Luther, Loyola, Calvin und die Europäische Neuzeit," 9.
3. Korbel, *Detente in Europe*, 30.
4. Murray, *Secret of Christ Our Life*.
5. Schwarz, *Method and Context as Problems for Contemporary Theology*, 37.
6. Garrett, *Problem of the Old Testament*, 7–8.

Introduction

Consequently, during this course, we shall study five different types of theologies: (1) Humanistic theology, which rediscovered the importance of the study of Scripture in its original languages, Greek and Hebrew, as well as ancient philosophy and humanistic studies in general,[7] (2) Lutheran theology, which rediscovered the importance of justification by faith alone,[8] (3) Reformed theology, which rediscovered the importance of God's sovereignty and predestination,[9] (4) Catholic theology, which rediscovered the importance of reforming ecclesiastical practice, fought against the Evangelicals, and reaffirmed Catholic doctrine,[10] and (5) Radical theology, which rediscovered the importance of adult baptism as well as the separation between church and state.[11]

Despite its complexity, Reformation theology is essentially practical in nature because it developed in the midst of the problems of daily life and its specific convulsions. For instance, Bruce Gordon, believes that the religious ideas of the Reformation grew to fruition in the middle of wars, persecutions, and plagues, so they developed within extreme social and intellectual instability. Thus, according to Gordon, the language used by Reformation theologians, Catholics and Protestants, is like a "brilliant prism"[12] which breaks a ray of light into multiple-colored beams; in other words, all Reformation theologians read the same Bible and the same gospel, but each explained them in his or her own way. Furthermore, each defended them with conviction in a way which can be defined as exclusivist; as it was often the case, some were so deeply convicted by their personal beliefs that did not even consider the views of other colleagues which were therefore severely criticized.

Berndt Moeller is sure that this is precisely what makes the Reformation so important, so it cannot be left in the care of systematic theologians alone. The Reformation, he writes, must be studied as history because otherwise it can be oversimplified and distorted. In fact, as far as Moeller is concerned, the Reformation had a powerful impact on history because it

---

7. Dost, *Renaissance Humanism in Support of the Gospel in Luther's Early Correspondence*, 62.

8. Stephenson, *Performing the Reformation*, 59.

9. Olson, *Story of Christian Theology*, 398.

10. Wright, *Counter-Reformation*, 20–22.

11. Kirby, *Persuasion and Conversion*, 26n62.

12. Gordon, "Changing Face of Protestant History and Identity in the Sixteenth Century."

unfolded within history, so theology, and especially Reformation theology, cannot and must not be detached from history.[13]

This is why Richard Muller says that Reformation theology must be studied with scientific honesty and integrity.[14] Thus, any intelligent theologian is capable of using Calvin's theology as he pleases, but only an honest theologian who is also a competent historian will listen to Calvin without using his theology for personal and confessional purposes.

Consequently, this course does not contain exclusively theological and dogmatic information but also some historical data which is supposed to balance the potentially faulty interpretations of Reformation theology. The balance between theology and history is mandatory within the context of Reformation studies because, as proven by Thomas Brady, professor of early modern history at the University of California at Berkeley, the Reformation represents the adaptation of Christianity to Europe's social and historical evolution, which requires a new approach to Reformation studies.[15]

Last but not least, as detailed by John O'Malley, the Reformation is a theological event which, although studied from a multitude of perspectives, must be thoroughly researched and analyzed from the perspective of its theological essence.[16] This is to say that the study of the Reformation should be devoid of confessional and ecclesiastical bias, even if such partisan studies are sadly present within the historiography which has investigated the issue of Reformation theology for the past five centuries.

It is therefore rather clear why Steven Ozment writes in one of his numerous works that the Reformation desperately needs a Moses who is supposed to guide her through the stormy seas of contemporary polemics.[17] Moreover, the Reformation must be reclaimed from social and intellectual history scholars because it must be studied within its original context. Thus, the Reformation must be analyzed, as honestly and scientifically as possible, within the setting in which it first appeared with reference to all the characters, ideas, and events that informed the sixteenth century.

---

13. Moeller, *Imperial Cities and the Reformation*, 16.
14. Muller, *Unaccommodated Calvin*, 188.
15. Brady, "Social History," 176.
16. O'Malley, *Trent and All That*, 45.
17. Ozment, *Religion and Culture in the Renaissance and Reformation*, 4.

Introduction

THE REFORMATION AND ITS THEOLOGIANS

The Reformation emerged as a pastoral event because of a set of pastoral and practical problems of the Catholic church, and not as a scientific debate within the university. In this specifically pastoral context, the Reformation attempted to bring the Catholic church back to its patristic roots as well as to the tradition of the early church with its belief in the *lex orandi, lex credendi* slogan which affirms the doxological foundation of faith in the sense that faith is deeply rooted in ecclesiastical worship. Thus, Jeffrey Meyers explains that the Reformation upholds "the absolute authority of the Bible over all other sources, including tradition" with all its historical and liturgical aspects.[18]

On the other hand, Alister McGrath shows that the Reformation took theology out of monasteries and universities, so that every theological endeavor became an issue of a new public consciousness dominated by an acute interest in all the practical problems of daily life.[19] As it came out of monasteries and universities, theology was suddenly being hotly debated as well as intensely argued about in the streets as well as in city councils. Reformation theology is extremely practical, and Paul Russell reveals that it captivates the attention of common people,[20] so Protestant doctrines were explained in such a way that everybody was capable of understanding what they were all about.

For instance, the issue of predestination was no longer considered an abstract problem; on the contrary, it became a manifestation of pastoral concern, so the theology of the Reformation succeeded in lifting the burden of salvation from the people's backs (as it was in the Catholic penitential doctrine). Even if predestination was often not preached in Lutheran circles because some people may get the wrong idea about God's dealings with humanity, as David Steinmetz notices,[21] this shift in theological thinking happened in order to place the burden of salvation back on Christ's shoulders where it belonged in the first place—as in the doctrines of forensic justification by faith alone, election, and effective calling, so ardently proclaimed within Reformed quarters. In this respect, Karl Barth shows that predestination is "the central Reformed doctrine" in close connection

---

18. Meyers, *Lord's Service*, 110.
19. McGrath, *Historical Theology*, 3.
20. Russell, *Lay Theology in the Reformation*, 77.
21. Steinmetz, *Reformers in the Wings*, 150.

with "effective calling, justification, acceptance, and sanctification" as "the implications of election."[22]

Reformation theology was successful not only because of its practical side but also because of the fundamental Evangelical conviction, highlighted by James Mead, that the word of God (the Bible) is always more important than the theologians' words about God or "the dogmatic theological statements of the church."[23] The personal and subjective reading of Scripture is always more important than anybody else's opinion. The Reformation theologians were never interested in objectivity and relevance because what really matters is the preaching of salvation based on God's word (which is the only genuine objectivity).

According to Timothy George, this concern for God's word was encapsulated by the Reformers in the phrase "the clarity of Scripture,"[24] which was both internal (the Spirit's illumination of the believer to understand Scripture) and external (the Spirit's inspiration of the human authors of Scripture to write it down as divine revelation). The Christian faith is totally irrelevant anyway as it is utterly implausible to those who do not know God personally. The Reformers were much more interested in the truth of God's promises found in Scripture than they were in the opinions of men, irrespective of how important these were in reality.

The Reformation was and still is an extremely complex and diverse process, although one can also speak of a unity which characterizes Reformation theology. Thus, this course will focus on the unique character of Reformation theology and especially on the doctrine of justification by faith alone, while all the other doctrines will be treated as secondary in nature despite their dogmatic and historical importance. This is why, in this course, the doctrine of justification by faith alone is considered to be not only the central aspect but also the ultimate limit of Reformation theology. Gerard Forde calls it "a matter of death and life today,"[25] as much as it was during the sixteenth century, while R. C. Sproul describes justification by faith alone as "essential to the gospel" and "essential for salvation."[26]

Carter Lindberg indicates that this perspective, which emphasizes the crucial importance of justification by faith alone as foundational Protestant

---

22. Barth, *Theology of the Reformed Confessions*, 136.
23. Mead, *Biblical Theology: Issues, Methods, and Themes*, 23.
24. George, *Reading Scripture with the Reformers*, 130.
25. Forde, *Justification by Faith*, 40.
26. Sproul, *Faith Alone*, 213.

doctrine, was promoted by Martin Brecht, professor of theology at the University of Münster, who was convinced that the essence of Luther's, Calvin's, and Zwingli's theology resided in justification by faith alone and the anthropology of justified people. Within the same vein, Berndt Hamm indicates that the foundation of Luther's, Calvin's, Zwingli's, and Melanchthon's religious thought is the very same doctrine of justification by faith alone.[27]

Reformation theology had a common agenda, as explained by Scott Hendrix.[28] All reformers shared the same desire to uproot the old medieval Catholic religion in order to plant a new one; moreover, both Protestant and Catholic theologians were in agreement that the old religion of the Late Middle Ages dominated by the rationalist scholasticism of those times had to be abandoned, although they failed to agree on how to practically apply this shared conviction.

Unfortunately, the Protestants were also highly unsuccessful in finding a common way to apply the new perspective on theology which resulted in confessionalization, a phenomenon that became characteristic of Protestantism from the very start. Not everything, however, is negative when it comes to confessionalization. Peter Leithard, for instance, seems persuaded that confessionalization is a process of dogmatic and ecclesiastical consolidation[29] within the broader spectrum of Protestant approaches to religion and theology.

This is why the theological controversies of the Reformation were extremely severe and intolerance was practiced both by Catholics and Protestants. Doctrinal fights were common, and their acute intensity caused Philip Melanchthon to say, as signaled by Andrew Kloes, that he often wished to die not only to escape his own sins, but also to eschew the madness of theologians, the infamous *rabies theologorum*.[30] Carlos M. N. Eire demonstrates that each reformer defended his or her opinions with such conviction that Luther once said about Andreas Bodenstein von Karlstadt that he must have swallowed the Holy Spirit "feathers and all";[31] as for Thomas Müntzer, as one can see in Jean Audin, Luther thought he was the devil incarnate.[32]

27. Lindberg, "Introduction," 7.
28. Hendrix, "Rerooting the Faith," 64.
29. Leithart, *End of Protestantism*.
30. Kloes, *German Awakening*, 22–23.
31. Eire, *Reformations*, 194.
32. Audin, *History of the Life, Writings, and Doctrines of Luther*, 2:15.

A Very Brief Introduction to Reformation Doctrine

According to Ozment, the very same Luther said that Melanchthon combined substance with eloquence, Erasmus showed eloquence without substance, while Karlstadt was capable of neither substance nor eloquence.[33] Thus, as we can read in William Naphy's excellent collection of Reformation documents, it is not surprising that, in writing to Martin Bucer, Erasmus confided in him that he just could not join the Reformers because of their endless fights and quarrels which were more than merely evident in the letters written by Luther, Zwingli, and Osiander against one another; Erasmus seems to have hated what Naphy calls "the tendency of the reforming to splinter."[34] It must be stressed here though that even if rude and often really impertinent, the Reformers' behavior stemmed not only from deep personal convictions, but also from their powerful desire to preach the gospel for the salvation of as many people as possible.

Given this situation, some reformers decided even to go back to the old Catholic church of Rome. In this respect, Erika Rummel reminds us of the peculiar case of Willibald Pirckheimer, who became famous for adhering to the Reformation only to leave it after a short while.[35] Thus, having joined Luther because he really hoped that the Church of Rome would recover from the charlatanism and thievery of monks and priests, Pirckheimer concluded that the situation became worse under the influence of Luther's new ideas.

Unfortunately, Luther's new ideas were not exactly appreciated by Calvin either. Erasmus Middleton, for instance, shows that in a letter to Heinrich Bullinger, Zwingli's successor in Zürich, Calvin wrote that Luther had a shameless character and was totally incapable of controlling his feelings. Moreover, Calvin was convinced that anyone who engages in any controversy with Luther will achieve nothing but useless strife and tragic fun for unbelievers. Despite this negative perspective, Calvin concluded his letter in a more positive tone by saying that Luther was nonetheless an extremely important person endowed with special spiritual gifts, even "an illustrious servant of God."[36]

Likewise, the humanists, whose top representative was Erasmus, were deeply dissatisfied with the Reformation. Edward Westermarck reveals the reason behind the humanists' scorn: the Evangelical ideas promoted by the

---

33. Ozment, *Age of Reform, 1250–1550*, 342n7.
34. Naphy, *Documents on the Continental Reformation*, 90.
35. Rummel, *Confessionalization of Humanism in Reformation Germany*, 81.
36. Middleton, *Biographia Evangelica*, 33.

first reformers, such as Luther and Zwingli, were notoriously unsuccessful in improving the morality of the vast majority of the sixteenth century's Europeans.[37]

Luther, however, was not interested in anything even remotely resembling a sudden change of morals. He was convinced that the Reformation did not consist of the ethical and moral regeneration of society but rather in preaching that salvation was received, not made by men and women. This is why Brad Gregory writes that such convictions, which often resulted in theological strife, "rendered any shared moral community impossible."[38]

Morality, however, was not the Reformer's primary concern. What they were really concerned about was the fact that the human being receives salvation directly from God himself, he does not work it based on its own efforts. Thus, Luther believed, justification only by faith, which always comes based on God's grace and benevolence, teaches us that discipleship does not and should not depend on its actual results. In the words of Ronald Rittgers, Luther's most fundamental conviction resided in the belief that "salvation is entirely in the hands of God" because "what saves a person" is "not self-made righteousness."[39]

In other words, in Luther, one must never give up because one's efforts yield negative results. Life is difficult among both Catholics and Evangelicals, and what really counts is right doctrine, without which morality is impossible. It is important for preaching to be correct in all respects and the teachings of Scriptures to be proclaimed as they were given by God in his word. "Right dogma mattered to Luther more than right living," Harry Loewen writes, and this is because, in Luther, "right conduct was not necessarily a sign of right doctrine."[40]

Luther was convinced that there is no genuine sanctification without right doctrine, coupled with the action of the Holy Spirit whose work of sanctification is complete only in the life to come. In this respect, Jared Wicks provides us with an illuminating image: in Luther, "holiness looks to its own eschatological perfection" because "the Spirit has begun his work and is pushing it forward."[41] Nobody is able to lead a life of holiness and

---

37. Westermarck, *Christianity and Morals*, 45.
38. Gregory, *Unintended Reformation*.
39. Rittgers, *Reformation of Suffering*, 97.
40. Loewen, *Luther and the Radicals*.
41. Wicks, *Luther's Reform*, 218.

morality without knowing the teachings which God gave us in the Holy Scripture through the work of the Holy Spirit.

ASSESSMENT QUESTIONS

1. What is Reformation theology?
2. How many types of Reformation theology are included in this course?
3. Should we study the Reformation as history?
4. What is the connection between holiness and doctrine in Reformation theology?
5. Does Reformation theology refer only to Protestantism?

2

Humanist Theology
Jacques Lefèvre d'Etaples and Desiderius Erasmus of Rotterdam

OBJECTIVES

1. To be aware of humanist Catholic theology which prepared the way for the Reformation;
2. To know humanist hermeneutics which led to the development of Protestant theologies;
3. To realize the importance of the study of Scripture in the original languages, especially that of the Greek New Testament;
4. To become acquainted with the dogmatic development of Christianity from Lefèvre's and Erasmus's Catholic humanism to Luther's early Protestantism;
5. To present some common aspects of Lefèvre's and Erasmus's Catholic humanism and Luther's early Protestantism.

Key words: Lefèvre, Erasmus, hermeneutics, Scripture, justification, will

JACQUES LEFÈVRE (1460-1536)

Interested in philosophy, medieval spirituality, patristic theology and the translation of Holy Scripture, Lefèvre was one of the first promoters of early

A Very Brief Introduction to Reformation Doctrine

biblical hermeneutics, the science which deals with the interpretation of Scripture. In this particular field, we learn from Philip Krey, Lefèvre writes about the Christocentric interpretation of Scripture by insisting that the literal meaning of the text,[1] namely the true meaning of Scripture is, in fact, a combination between the literal and the spiritual meaning. Thus, according to Lefèvre, the literal meaning is the interpretation discovered by the Holy Spirit, a fact Jonathan A. Reid notices in his discussion about Lefèvre's hermeneutics.[2]

In so doing Lefèvre detaches himself from medieval commentaries which defend the so-called fourfold meaning of Scripture (*quadriga*) inclusive of the following interpretative categories, as we can see in Peter Harrison's explanation regarding this reading method of the Bible during the Middle Ages: (1) the literal-historical meaning or the facts we read about, (2) the allegorical meaning or what we should believe by faith, (3) the tropological meaning or what we should do morally by hope, and (4) the anagogical meaning or what we should strive for by love.[3]

Richard Soulen provides a brief but illuminating image of how the *quadriga* works exegetically. If the literal-historical meaning is the result of the normal reading of the biblical text and contains the ideas which are obvious in Scripture, the allegorical meaning forces the reader to search for a more abstract interpretation within the words of the text, which can be discovered only by faith. Beyond this, however, the tropological meaning supports a kind of moral reading, which is actually the final purpose of Scripture, namely the desire to achieve a radically changed moral life that can be lived out only through Christian love. Last, the anagogic meaning pushes the reading towards a more mystical interpretation which can be deciphered by means of hope or, more precisely, the hope inspired by Christ himself; so the three theological virtues of faith, hope, and love lie at the very foundation of the *quadriga* as "spiritual senses" aimed at a reflexive approach of the Bible.[4] Thus, the medieval *quadriga* focuses on a certain reading of Scripture which combines philology with theology and ethics, because the understanding of the biblical text entails the acceptance and application of scriptural teachings in everyday life.

---

1. Krey, "Lefèvre d'Etaples, Jacques (c. 1455–1536)," 206.
2. Reid, *King's Sister—Queen of Dissent*, 127.
3. Harrison, *Bible, Protestantism, and the Rise of Natural Science*, 26–27.
4. Soulen, *Sacred Scripture*, 99.

Humanist Theology

Lefèvre believes that Scripture must have a singular meaning, both literal and spiritual, which must lead to a christological reading of the Bible because, as Tadataka Maruyama is keen to emphasize, Christ is the spirit of the whole Scripture.[5] Without Christ, Scripture is merely just another writing, namely it is nothing more than just the letter which kills. The Holy Spirit, however, does not leave the world linger in darkness, Lefèvre believes, but preaches all the mysteries of Christ who is the only truth. Robert Kolb insists that, in Lefèvre, the Bible can be read only christologically[6] for Christ is the mediator who opens up Scripture before our eyes so that all of us understand it. Likewise, the Bible is a collection of books that are united by Christ, and it is in this capacity that Scripture talks about the Word (*logos*), which is Christ. This christological reading of Scripture allows Lefèvre to present Christ as mediator, the only person capable of reconciling us with God, as well as truth, which is why Scripture cannot be read but christologically.

One of Lefèvre's main preoccupations was the doctrine of justification which he first presented as having a double composition. Thus, according to Willem van 't Spijker, Lefèvre believed that there was a justification of the law which worked by good deeds and a justification of faith which worked by grace.[7] The human being, however, said Lefèvre, must look for both, and especially for the justification of faith because this is preferred by the Gospels while the justification of the law is pursued mainly by philosophers. Later, Lefèvre wrote that there is only one justification, which he calls universal. It must be underlined here, as we can see in Catharine Randall, that Lefèvre uses the phrase *sola gratia* (by grace alone) numerous times, as he was convinced that each believer must receive and accept God's grace through faith (*sola fide*), ideas which deeply impacted the Reformation.[8]

Consequently, in his thought, the human being's blessedness and happiness is not based on good deeds, but only on God's grace and benevolence. Eric Ives is of the opinion that, in Lefèvre, salvation is impossible if human beings cling to their good works.[9] Good deeds are necessary for the preparation and the growth of justification, and idea which Luther rejected in categorical terms a little later, because, as Lefèvre points out, without

---

5. Maruyama, *Calvin's Ecclesiology*.
6. Kolb, *Martin Luther as He Lived and Breathed*, 39.
7. Van 't Spijker, *Calvin*, 6.
8. Randall, *Earthly Treasures*, 291n4.
9. Ives, *Reformation Experience*, 81.

good deeds the human being forsakes the grace of justification. Nevertheless, in Lefèvre, the good deeds performed without faith and only based on human love cannot be counted as good deeds. Thus, Philip Hughes writes that, in Lefèvre's theology, the believer must embrace both the necessity of grace like Paul and the necessity of good deeds like James because the principle at work in salvation is "forgiveness through grace."[10] The Scripture is clear, Lefèvre indicates, and it is also consistent because of this, so there are no contradictions between Paul and James, between grace and good deeds. Lefèvre's mistake consists of placing good deeds before justification, so in his theology good deeds are the cause of justification, not the other way around as it was in the theology of the early Protestant reformers. In the end though, according to Lefèvre, the human being must place his confidence in God, not in faith or in works:

> There were two parties in times past: one which focused on works and another one on faith without paying attention to works. James rejects the latter, while Paul the former. You, however, if you do have the wisdom of the Spirit, put your trust neither in faith, nor in works, but in God; because what you must consider essential in order to obtain God's salvation is faith according to Paul but do add to this the works according to James since these are the sign of a faith which is living and productive.[11]

Another preoccupation in Lefèvre's thought is sacramental theology, especially the doctrines of baptism and the Lord's Supper. Jonathan Arnold points out that for Lefèvre baptism was the washing of the new birth,[12] and it stands not only for the forgiveness of sins but also for holiness which is our adoption in Christ and our reconciliation with God in Christ. Baptism must be performed by triple immersion, which symbolizes the work of the Holy Trinity as well as the three days Christ spent in the tomb. The baptism of Christ is the cleansing, justification, and sanctification of believers who make up the church as born again or regenerated people. The Eucharist is the believer's food for eternal life and the remembrance of Christ's sacrifice on the cross. It is crucial to see here that, although a Catholic, Lefèvre does not mention transubstantiation, but he insists on the importance of grace leading to faith, not on receiving the sacrament as in Catholic dogma. As

---

10. Hughes, *Lefèvre*, 76.
11. De Sabatier-Plantier, *Rôle de Jacques Lefèvre d'Etaples*, 22.
12. Arnold, *Great Humanists*, 214.

far as Darwell Stone is concerned, in Lefèvre, the Eucharist is a "memorial of the one sacrifice of Christ" for the "benefit of the soul."[13]

A vital issue in Lefèvre's theology is homiletics because sermons, he points out, must present Scripture to all believers, they must combine faith, hope, and love, as well as help the human being search for God's mysteries. The believer must learn from sermons; he must learn how to follow Christ, how to grow in Christ's likeness, and how to take Christ's shape (Christomorphism) by focusing on Christ himself (Christocentrism). Lefèvre's conviction is based on what the apostle Paul said in Galatians 2:20, that the Christian no longer lives by himself but Christ lives within him; in Carlos Eire's words: "Lefèvre proposed an intense Christocentrism. Jesus Christ, the word of God made flesh, was to be the central point of reference in the life of the church."[14]

This is why the human being must look for God's mysteries, because the Holy Spirit illuminates the preacher as well as those who listen to the sermon. T. H. L. Parker notices that, in Lefèvre, "the mysticism was... the key with which he unlocked the Scriptures."[15] In his homilies, Lefèvre did not mention the sacraments, the invocation of saints or the ecclesiastical hierarchy, but he rather insisted on God's word as foundation for all believers. God's true house, however, is not the church as much as it is the human heart, soul, and mind, and it is in this house that God teaches us how he wants to be served by prayer. It is also in this house that God teaches us how to worship him in spirit and truth. In Lefèvre, however, adequate worship can only be performed—as underlined by Richard Hannula—by thanking Christ and obeying his commandments.[16]

DESIDERIUS ERASMUS (1469–1536)

Famous for his *Praise of Folly* as well as for his Greek New Testament and its Latin translation and commentaries, Erasmus is one of the most important Christian humanists—Stefan Zweig, for instance, writes that Erasmus is: "the greatest and most brilliant star of his century."[17] A Catholic throughout his life despite some very close connections with the Protestant Reformation,

13. Stone, *History of the Doctrine of the Holy Eucharist*, 7.
14. Eire, *War Against the Idols*, 173.
15. Parker, *John Calvin*, 13.
16. Hannula, *Heralds of the Reformation*, 120.
17. Zweig, *Erasmus of Rotterdam*.

he was deeply interested in the study of Scripture but also in Greek and Latin philosophy which he considered vital for any genuine theologians. Moreover, Erasmus was convinced that the writings of Greek and Latin philosophers were mandatory for preachers because the latter were utterly incapable of improving their language without the former. Getting the meaning of the text was extremely important for Erasmus, especially about the Bible; Hughes Oliphant Old points out that, in Erasmus, paraphrases were preferred to "straightforward translation" if they were better in conveying the meaning of the biblical text.[18]

As far as Erasmus is concerned, there is an obvious connection between the quality of the language used by the preacher and the correct understanding of the message by the listener. Christians, he believed, inherited the necessary instruments for a correct understanding of the gospel from Greek and Latin philosophers. Thus, the reading of Scripture, combined with the study of Greek and Latin literature and philosophy, does assist the believer in better understanding Christ's way. Russ Leo explains that, according to Erasmus, any person can be a theologian provided he or she understands Christ and his true theology.[19] In other words, any person who knows Greek and Latin philosophy can, at least in theory, become a Christian. This is why Erasmus was deeply convinced that some of the pagan philosophers would be accepted in heaven because of the moral quality of their lives, and a good example in this respect was Socrates. In Erasmus, the reading of Scripture allows us to understand what God wants from us, but it is compulsory for us to know how to read the Scripture in order for us to properly understand it. In rejecting scholastic theology and its rationalism, as István Bejczy correctly notices, Erasmus demonstrated an evident preference for the allegorical meaning of Scripture (like Origen, Ambrose, Jerome, and Augustin) to the detriment of its literal counterpart.[20]

This allegorical and philosophical reading of Scripture caused Erasmus to present the Christian faith as a philosophy, which he described as the philosophy of Christ. Such a christological philosophy, Ross Dealy writes, "demanded a personal approach to the Gospel and increased familiarity with its message" and this is precisely why Erasmus advocated "a return to the sources."[21] He firmly believed that this was the only true philosophy,

---

18. Old, *Reading and Preaching of the Scriptures*, 4:70.
19. Leo, *Tragedy as Philosophy in the Reformation World*, 107.
20. Bejczy, *Erasmus and the Middle Ages*, 77.
21. Dealy, *Stoic Origins of Erasmus' Philosophy of Christ*, 54.

not medieval scholastic rationalism. Christ's philosophy is vital for all human beings because everything, the whole creation, all the things that exist point to Christ. Thus, Lucy Razzall demonstrates that, for Erasmus, Christ is the teacher who came from heaven, he is the eternal wisdom and the only maker of our eternal salvation who gives us his heavenly treasures.[22] Christ alone can fulfill what he promised, he alone can save us all if we truly want to know him. The knowledge of Christ is possible only through the reading of Scripture since Scripture has the ability to explain divine things to human beings in a way which is easy to comprehend an appealing to further study:

> The Scripture has a style and language which should diligently be considered. The divine wisdom stoops to the level of our capacities, as a fond mother lisps to her children. It tenders milk to babes in Christ, strong meat to the adult. It condescends to our weakness, and we should rise to its sublimity. It would be absurd to be always a child, and idle to make no proficiency.[23]

It is rather obvious that Erasmus had an optimistic perspective on human nature which led him to believe that Greek and Latin philosophy can be useful to all Christians because it teaches them about Christ's philosophy. Thus, Christine Christ-von Wedel believes, that, in Erasmus, Christ's philosophy presupposes the restoration of human nature to its original state, namely to the state it had when it was created by God.[24] The human being has an extremely important role in receiving God's grace, so he can work for his own salvation. In this respect, educated and elevated language is crucial for the transmission of God's love. According to Garon Wheeler, Erasmus's core pedagogical conviction was that "the basis of all education rests upon a mastery of language,"[25] and that includes theological education and religious instruction. In Erasmus, therefore, one's salvation depends ultimately on the preacher's education or lack thereof.

The preacher, however, speaks about Christ and in order for us to understand Christ we must read the Scriptures; there is no other way to know Christ without reading the Bible. In this respect, Paul A. Russell writes that "Erasmus sees Christ as the substantial gift of meditation on Scripture who

---

22. Razzall, *Boxes and Books in Early Modern England*, 133.
23. Erasmus, *Christian's Manual*, 30.
24. Christ-von Wedel, *Erasmus of Rotterdam*, 119.
25. Wheeler, *Language Teaching through the Ages*, 44.

accomplishes a conversion of the human heart."[26] In concrete terms, the Christ incarnate in the Bible is the same with the Christ incarnate on earth because Christ was a genuine human being and he suffered like any other human being. As we can see in Kirk Essary, Erasmus frequently stressed the fact that Jesus was a poor man,[27] a carpenter nobody cared about, but despite this he was truly God. Christ's poverty, Erasmus believes, indicates that Jesus rejected the values of the world, so those who want to be commended by the world will never understand Christ's sacrifice on the cross.

Christ's crucifixion, on the other hand, teaches us that God's madness if wise than man's madness because nobody would have ever thought that such an action might lead to the salvation of the entire human race. Sam Hall believes that, in Erasmus, "God's primary folly is the incarnation" but "by the standards of worldly logic, this action, through which the immortal became mortal, is foolish or even man."[28] Salvation, however, can be seen, and in the church, this is possible through the mediation provided by the sacraments which are signs of grace, not causes of grace. In Erasmus's theology, sacraments are both physical and spiritual, even if Erasmus is always more inclined to underline the spiritual side in his commentaries. Thus, infant baptism is valid, but it must always be accompanied by sanctification, while marriage must never be considered inferior to celibacy; on the contrary, as we read in Philip Reynolds, Erasmus even argued "that the married estate was superior to celibacy."[29] All these convictions originated in the study of the New Testament, especially in the Greek original, and it was this activity which provided Erasmus with worldwide notoriety.

One of the most famous episodes in Erasmus's life is his theological controversy with Luther which had to do with free will. Erasmus believed that the will was free, an idea Luther dismissed without equivocation, and he did so, Miikka Ruokanen contends, by accusing Erasmus "of using mere rhetoric to deceive his readers."[30] While Erasmus was convinced that the human being had the power to do something for his salvation based on his capacity to freely use his will because, as demonstrated by Gregory Graybill, he was "readier to attempt rational explanations of difficult doctrines,"[31] Lu-

26. Russell, *Lay Theology in the Reformation*, 76.
27. Essary, *Erasmus and Calvin on the Foolishness of God*, 97.
28. Hall, *Shakespeare's Folly*, 25.
29. Reynolds, *How Marriage Became One of the Sacraments*, 731.
30. Ruokanen, *Trinitarian Grace in Martin Luther's* The Bondage of the Will, 173.
31. Graybill, *Evangelical Free Will*, 54.

ther was adamant about the fact that there was no such thing as a free will since the reality of sin affected all the aspects of the human being.

As far as Erasmus was concerned, things were clear: by the power of his will, which is the very essence of free will, a fact Eddie Mabry competently underlines,[32] the human being can at least head towards eternal salvation even if he needed help every step of the way through God's grace, which is a fourfold reality: (1) natural grace (by which God helps us exist despite sin), (2) operative grace (by which God helps us repent), (3) cooperative grace (by which God helps us become justified based on good deeds), and (4) perfect grace (by which God helps us remain under the power of Christ). The last three, which have to do with salvation, can be accepted freely or rejected according to Erasmus because in his thought, we are told by Donald Gelpi, the human will has this discerning capacity.[33]

Frederick Kiefer investigated the conflict between Erasmus and Luther, which spanned across many years. Erasmus received an extremely critical answer from Luther who, despite being grateful to Erasmus for his contribution to biblical languages, still compared Erasmus's fate (in not joining the Reformation) to Moses's death in Moab (Erasmus's failure to move from philology to theology).[34] In his critique of Erasmus, Luther underlined four aspects: (1) the human being has no free will because sin damages his entire created nature, (2) the human being does not possess the kind of righteousness which enables him to choose freely, (3) the human being cannot choose freely or correctly because of the damages produced by sin, and (4) the human being can only accept and receive God's grace because any other human action is irreparably damaged by sin. Thus, Greta Kroker is right in saying that, for Luther, "the very heart of the Gospel and therefore of the reform of theology and the church" was "the freedom of the will"[35] and all that was brought to the fore by Erasmus's defense of this crucial aspect of human psychology.

ASSESSMENT QUESTIONS

1. What does Lefèvre say about justification?

---

32. Mabry, *Balthasar Hubmaier's Understanding of Faith*, 69.
33. Gelpi, *Gracing of Human Experience*, 91.
34. Kiefer, *Writing on the Renaissance Stage*, 32.
35. Kroeker, *Erasmus in the Footsteps of Paul*, 18–19.

2. What does Lefèvre say about Bible reading?
3. How should the Bible be studied according to Erasmus?
4. Is there free will in Erasmus's theology?
5. Are there any resemblances between Lefèvre's and Erasmus's Catholic theology and Luther's early theology?

3

Lutheran Theology (1)
Martin Luther and Philip Melanchthon

OBJECTIVES

1. To understand the concept of theology in Luther's thought;
2. To learn about the theology of creation in Luther's thought;
3. To comprehend the most important doctrines in Luther's theology;
4. To identify the main doctrines in Melanchthon's theology;
5. To know the doctrine of justification in Melanchthon's theology.

Key words: Luther, Melanchthon, justification, church, will, sin

MARTIN LUTHER (1483–1546)

Luther begins his Reformation efforts through a radical redefinition of the concept of theology. Thus, in criticizing medieval scholastic theology dominated by strict rationalism, Luther writes that Christian theology should be a theology of the cross (*theologia crucis*), a theology whose essence is wisdom rooted in experience (*sapientia experimentalis*). This exercise, Brian Gerrish writes, shows that "Luther permitted Scripture to criticize tradition, not merely to support it; and he asserted the rights of well-founded personal interpretation of scripture against the traditional interpretation held by the church."[1]

---
1. Gerrish, *Continuing the Reformation*, 54.

In order to do this, however, theology must be constantly informed by prayer, meditation, and trials, even suffering, while the core of this particular theology is justification by faith, as we read in Oswald Bayer's presentation of Luther's take on faith as "venture" and "boldness."[2] In Luther's thought, theology is based on a passive faith—bold enough to rely on God's promises, as Kirsi Stjerna writes[3]—which means that the human being can only receive salvation from God so he cannot acquire it on his own, by his own efforts, attempts, and deeds, be those even good deeds.

Thus, Scott Hafermann thinks that, in Luther, the believer's life is passive (*vita passiva*), not active as in medieval theology where the human being does have a role in obtaining salvation; but the believer's faith "is active... in love."[4] Theology, Luther believes, should never be a scientific or university endeavor, but rather a pastoral effort in which theology should be constantly based on the foundation provided by the word of God. Such a theology will always entertain the relationship between the human being and God as its subject, a relationship in which the human being is sinful while God is holy.

The human being cannot receive salvation from anyone but God; this is why the human being is passive in the salvation process while God is active. In Luther's view, without faith in Christ the human being is able to see God only as enemy. Such a human being is what Luther calls *homo nudus*, a man or a woman stripped of faith who can see God only as *Deus nudus*, a God stripped of love, a hidden and utterly inaccessible God (*Deus absconditus*). In this respect, Gerrit Berkouwer insists that Luther's *Deus absconditus* is meant to clarify revelation by contrasting it with *Deus revelatus*, not to cast relativistic shadow over it.[5]

Then, without faith in Christ, the human being fights against God because he cannot understand him. When faith eventually dwells within the human being, he begins to see God as his savior. This particular human being is what Luther identifies as *homo justificatus*, namely a person who is considered righteous, pure, and innocent despite his sins, and who now is capable of seeing God as he is in reality, namely as he is revealed in the Holy Scripture (*Deus revelatus*). Rudolf Otto thinks that Luther's

---

2. Bayer, *Living by Faith*, 26.
3. Stjerna, *Lutheran Theology*, 73.
4. Hafemann, *Paul: Servant of the New Covenant*, 49.
5. Berkouwer, *Divine Election*, 128.

homo justificatus is a person who became one with God by giving his soul to Christ through faith.[6]

Thus, by faith in Christ, the human being understands that God alone can save him because, in his natural state dominated by sin, the human being cannot save himself. This is why, in Luther, faith makes God (*fides facit Deum*), it paints God exactly how he is, for the very simple reason that God can be truly known by faith alone on the basis of Scripture. As Ingolf Dalferth put it: "there is no way of determining what is conveyed without reference to its appropriation."[7] In other words, Luther's reasoning goes like this: there is no way of knowing how God is without reference to faith, which makes God before our eyes as trinity when we look at Christ and his humanity as portrayed in Scripture by the Spirit with utmost clarity:

> The Scripture simply confesses the trinity of God, the humanity of Christ, and the unpardonable sin. There is nothing here of obscurity or ambiguity. But how these things are, the Scripture does not say, nor is it necessary to be known . . . The Spirit is required to understand the whole of the Scripture and every part of it . . . All things that are in the Scriptures, are by the Word brought fort into the clearest light, and proclaimed to the whole world.[8]

A vital aspect of Luther's theology is the link between law and gospel, and this relationship must be deciphered by taking into account that God's justice (*justitia Dei*) is the very cause of our salvation and justification. Jairzinho Pereira reveals that, in Luther, God's justice was the reality that allowed him to save us.[9] The human being has no righteousness of his own; the human being only has sins, so God's intervention is needed for salvation to start as a real process in the human being's life. God therefore imputes Christ's righteousness to the human being, namely he considers the human being innocent of sins based on Christ's righteousness even if the human being is and remains sinful.

The Scripture explains rather plainly that the human being cannot fulfill the law, so the law leads inevitably to death. The gospel, however, namely the good news of Christ's salvation, leads to life because Christ's righteousness alone is able to save the human being. This is why the gospel

---

6. Otto, *West-Östliche Mystik*, 274.
7. Dalferth, *Crucified and Resurrected*.
8. Luther, *Martin Luther on the Bondage of the Will*, 16–17.
9. Pereira, *Augustine of Hippo and Martin Luther on Original Sin and Justification of the Sinner*, 298.

is God's word, namely Scripture, and this is full of God's promises. According to David Brondos, the gospel explains that the human being is justified, namely he is considered righteous and innocent exclusively by his faith in all God's promises,[10] so justification means to consider a person righteous or innocent, not to make a person righteous or innocent.

Nonetheless, this process unfolds in Luther's theology within the context of creation which, according to Risto Saarinen, is God's gift to the human being as well as to the church.[11] Through creation, God provides the human being with a vital space for life. God, Luther underlines, does not withdraw from creation, but he gets involved in its life, and for this God enters a relationship with the human being and he eventually saves him from his sins. In Luther's thought, creation exists in a threefold status: (1) the church (*status ecclesiasticus*), the fundamental state of humankind in which the human being must exist in a close relationship to God; (2) the home, the household or the family (*status oecomenicus*), which should be a part of the church because even though the human being does live in the world, the Christian must live in the world as part of the church; (3) the state (*status politicus*) which exists only because of sin and is mandated by God to punish the sins of human beings by using the sword, namely by implementing the punitive measures accepted by law. As we read in Thomas Kaufmann, in this threefold status defined by Luther,[12] the human being exists in a certain relationship to God regardless of whether he likes it or not or whether he is aware of it or not.

In this relationship to God, the human being enters in his capacity as God's image. Stanley Grenz mentions that this is how the human being also lives in the world between the fall, or his sin, and restoration, or the salvation mediated christologically and pneumatologically.[13] Thus, Luther explains, the human being is endowed by God with language and reason in order for him to rule the world and all the creatures in the world. The image of God therefore presupposes and contains human reason, language, and the rule or the authority over the whole of creation.

Reason is a divine reality which is deeply affected by sin within the human being, so faith must choke and suppress reason by forcing it into God's service. Reason must be subjugated by faith because of sin which began to

---

10. Brondos, *Redeeming the Gospel*, 53.
11. Saarinen, *Luther and the Gift*, 242.
12. Kaufmann, *Short Life of Martin Luther*, 77–78.
13. Grenz, *Social God and the Relational Self*, 165.

be active through the human being's rejection of what he was supposed to be (*peccatus omissionis*), which was followed by a concrete reprehensible action (*peccatus comissionis*) such as disobedience to God. Samuel Torvend gives an example used by Luther to illustrate this duality of sin especially with reference to wealthy people who can sin by omission when they do not help the poor or by commission when they plot against the poor with the intent to rob them.[14]

Thus, in Luther, sin is the lack of gratitude and the perversion of the created order, including that of human nature. Through sin—and, as Helmut Puff aptly proves, Luther often alluded to sexual sin[15]—the world is turned upside down and is thrown into darkness, Luther contends. Because human nature is affected by sin, the human will is also enslaved by sin. The human being cannot even want to be saved, so he needs the help of God's mercy which manifests itself by God's decision to send Christ to die for me, as Luther used to say, but also for all of us (*Christus pro me, Christus pro nobis*). Timothy George describes *Christus pro me* as "the heart of Luther's theology,"[16] while Bernd Hamm says of *Christus pro nobis* that it evokes man "being taken into . . . the exemplary Christ."[17] God enters history and human life through Christ's incarnation, while through Christ's death, he gives himself without reservation to all human beings because of his mercy and love. Luther insists on the fact that the human being is capable of knowing God's mercy and love by faith in Christ alone.

Faith is therefore the glue which keeps the church together, which is God's people and is sanctified by the Holy Spirit. In its capacity as God's people, the church is the gathering of the saints, the communion of those who were predestined for faith and good works. According to David Courey, Luther explains that in every human being faith comes through the hearing of the Word or *ex auditu*[18] and leads to good works, not the other way around.

In Luther's theology, faith is always the cause of good works, not the consequence thereof. The human being is freed from sins, and it is only in this particular state that he is capable of doing good works as proof of his justification. Good works are always the necessary and mandatory

---

14. Torvend, *Luther and the Hungry Poor*, 76.
15. Puff, *Sodomy in Reformation Germany and Switzerland, 1400–1600*, 138.
16. George, *Theology of the Reformers*, 60.
17. Hamm, *Early Luther*, 140.
18. Courey, *What Has Wittenberg to Do with Azusa?*, 128.

consequence of the faith of justified men and women, not its cause; as Joshua Furnal put it, good works are the "result" of faith and, implicitly, of justification by faith.[19]

PHILIP MELANCHTHON (1497–1560)

One of Luther's closest coworkers and friends, Melanchthon supported the head of the German Reformation in promoting the Protestant ideas, which in the sixteenth century were known as Evangelical, mainly by the publication of his *Loci communes* (Fundamental Principles), the very first book of Protestant systematic theology. This is why Barbara Pitkin describes Melanchthon as "the author of the first systematic explanation of evangelical theology," a book which "grew out of lectures on Romans" and that turns Melanchthon also in "the first Protestant to publish a commentary on Romans."[20] Melanchthon beings with the relationship between law and gospel by insisting that the correct understanding of the gospel depends on how we define the law. The gospel is God's gift, but the law is God's impossible standard, a standard nobody can meet. Thus, H. Ashley Hall is supportive of the fact that, in Melanchthon, the gospel reveals God's love and mercy which always goes far beyond the law.[21]

When he began his theological career, Melanchthon was in full agreement with Luther on the fact that the human being does not possess free will in matters pertaining to salvation which he can neither obtain nor wish for without the active guidance of the Holy Spirit. Timothy Wengert writes that, in the early stages of his theological career, Melanchthon was convinced that any attempt to support the doctrine of free would undermine "the entire doctrine of justification."[22]

Nevertheless, towards the end of his activity and also after Luther's death, Melanchthon was convinced that the human being does have a certain degree of freedom with respect to his will. This kind of synergism caused Melanchthon to defend the idea that the human being is not only capable of rejecting evil but also of doing good. Joshua Miller indicates that it is possible to trace Melanchthon's support of free will as early as "his 1532

---

19. Furnal, *Catholic Theology after Kierkegaard*, 21.
20. Pitkin, *Calvin, the Bible, and History*, 60.
21. Hall, *Philip Melanchthon and the Cappadocians*, 19.
22. Wengert, *Human Freedom, Christian Righteousness*, 1997.

Commentary on Romans" which continued through "his revisions of the *Loci communes*" as late as 1559, the year before his death.[23]

This anthropological optimism, similar to that displayed by Erasmus, profoundly influenced Melanchthon who, very much like Erasmus himself, recommended the study of Greek and Latin philosophy for a better understanding of theology, although not also for a more effective preaching of the gospel, as in was the case with Erasmus. According to Melanchthon, philosophy is important also for a better grasp of the moral law, which is encapsulated in the Ten Commandments and constitutes the very foundation of Christian ethics. Bruce Watke and James Houston go as far as to substantiate the idea that "Melanchthon later asserts that one could not exercise faith without Aristotle,"[24] which indicates his appreciation of philosophy as investigative instrument of theology. Moral philosophy is part of God's law which must reflect itself in every human action, including the educational system. This is why Melanchthon drafted a university curriculum which not only included philosophy, as George Marsden demonstrates,[25] but also proved to be so beneficial to education in German lands that Hans-Georg Gadamer recognized its influence through Joachim Camerarius, Melanchthon's student.[26]

Nevertheless, the seriousness of learning depends to a great extent on the doctrine of justification which in Melanchthon is forensic, as shown by Bruce McCormack, namely it is decided upon *in foro divino*, before the divine tribunal,[27] within the Holy Trinity itself. In Melanchthon, justification means that God considers the sinner righteous, or innocent of sins, without making him righteous. Justification becomes effective by faith alone (*sola fide*), only on the foundation provided by God's grace (*sola gratia*).

The human being possesses no merits for justification; God therefore works by the imputation of Christ's merits and righteousness to the sinful believer. Christ's righteousness is external to the sinner, so it comes from outside (*extra nos*) as "the basis of our justification," as Wengert writes,[28] but it becomes internal to the sinner as well as to all of us, by faith alone on

---

23. Miller, *Hanging by a Promise*, 43.
24. Waltke et al., *Psalms as Christian Worship*, 427.
25. Marsden, *Soul of the American University*, 36.
26. Gadamer, *Hans-Georg Gadamer on Education, Poetry, and History*, 26.
27. McCormack, *Justification in Perspective*, 101.
28. Wengert, *Defending Faith*, 196.

virtue of God's decision to impute Christ's righteousness on all those who believe. In Melanchthon's own words:

> Also they teach that men cannot be justified before God by their own strength, merits, or works, but are freely justified for Christ's sake, through faith, when they believe that they are received into favor, and that their sins are forgiven for Christ's sake, who, by his death, has made satisfaction for our sins. This faith God imputes for righteousness in his sight, Romans 3 and 4.[29]

Faith is seen not only in the life of every believer, but also in the life of the church which has two signs of grace or sacraments, as they were known since the time of the early church: baptism and the Lord's Supper. Amy Nelson Burnett insists that while Melanchthon wrote more on baptism than he did on the Lord's Supper, both feature saliently in his theology as "sacramental signs."[30] In their capacity as signs of grace instituted by God, the sacraments are effective by faith alone. In fact, as we are told by John Oyer, Melanchthon insists that in order for them to be effective, the sacraments need faith because they "signified God's gracious will toward men."[31] The Lord's Supper reminds us of Christ's sacrifice, so it does not presuppose the actual sacrifice of Christ during the liturgy every time the church celebrates it, as in the Catholic theology of the Roman church.

Each believer must partake at the Lord's Supper with repentance because Christ is present at the Eucharist in a real and substantial way. According to Ralph Quere, in Melanchthon, Christ is present in the sacrament "efficaciously, personally, and substantially."[32] Thus, at the Supper, believers remember Christ's work on the cross, his sacrifice, the forgiveness of sins due to Christ's righteousness, his resurrection from the dead, and the fact that Christ keeps us all in the church through his grace. Melanchthon's theology of the Lord's Supper developed in time because if in 1530 (in *Confessio Augustana Invariata*) he was in agreement with Luther (Christ is present in bread and wine in a real and substantial way), by 1540 (in *Confessio Augustana Variata*) he shared Calvin's perspective on the Eucharist, that Christ is present in bread and wine in a real and spiritual way. Despite this connection, Kilian McDonnel states that "it would be difficult to attribute much influence to Melanchthon in the area of Calvin's eucharistic

---

29. Melanchthon, *Augsburg Confession*, Article 4.
30. Nelson Burnett, *Debating the Sacraments*, 68.
31. Oyer, *Lutheran Reformers against Anabaptists*, 145.
32. Quere, *Melanchthon's Christum Cognoscere*, 384.

doctrine";[33] the resemblances, however, between Melanchthon and Calvin with regard to eucharistic theology are likely to remain a subject of dogmatic investigation.

Reinhold Seeberg reminds us of the crucial aspect that baptism and the Lord's Supper are not only administered but also instituted for believers,[34] and they also become effective only in those who really believe in Christ. In Melanchthon thus, the sacraments become effective only in the gathering of the holy, where the Son of God works powerfully through the gospel. The church is made perfect only in Christ because believers are, according to Augustine, a *corpus permixtum*, namely a gathering of people who are equally and simultaneously sinful and justified. According to Paul Avis, "Melanchthon never denied the mixed and imperfect nature of the church,"[35] but he was preoccupied with finding a proper definition for it. In order for the gathering of believers to be considered church, the community needs to display three distinct signs which are always genuine: (1) the correct preaching of the gospel, the correct administration of the sacraments, and (3) the obedience of the faithful to the work of the gospel.

In Melanchthon, true believers are holy because, as John Fesko writes, "God . . . gives to believers the Holy Spirit and eternal life."[36] In other words, believers continue to live in a general state of holiness even if they remain affected by sin for the rest of their lives. This is the true church, not the ecclesiastical hierarchy in Rome, and its unity is always provided by the foundation of faith in Christ and by the gospel of Christ, not by church councils. Every believer has the duty to know God and cultivate human communion, while the spiritual sanity of believers consists of a life of active prayer in all the stages of one's existence.

This ecclesiastical reality should characterize the church with all its believers regardless of whether they go through happiness or trouble, because the purpose of life is ultimately the contemplation of God and his Son. John Platt makes an important point when he explains that, in Melanchthon, the contemplation of God is facilitated by the existence of the universe: contemplating the universe as creation leads to contemplating God as creator.[37]

33. McDonnell, *John Calvin, the Church, and the Eucharist*, 102.
34. Seeberg, *Text-Book of the History of Doctrines*, 366.
35. Avis, *Church in the Theology of the Reformers*, 28.
36. Fesko, *Beyond Calvin*, 147.
37. Platt, *Reformed Thought and Scholasticism*, 23.

ASSESSMENT QUESTIONS

1. Which is the threefold status of creation in Luther's theology?
2. Which is the relationship between law and gospel in Luther?
3. Is there any causality between sin and enslaved will in Luther's theology?
4. How is justification presented in Melanchthon's theology?
5. Which are the signs of the church in Melanchthon's theology?

4

Lutheran Theology (2)
Matthias Flacius and Argula von Grumbach

OBJECTIVES

1. To familiarize with the theology of Matthias Flacius and his efforts to include Lutheran theology within ecclesiastical history;
2. To recognize Flacius's arguments for the continuity between Lutheran and Catholic theologies;
3. To understand Flacius's arguments for the resemblances between Lutheran and Eastern Orthodox theologies;
4. To become acquainted with modern hermeneutics as promoted by Flacius;
5. To know the foundational aspects of practical theology as promoted by Argula von Grumbach.

Key words: Flacius, Argula, justification, Scripture, Christ

MATTHIAS FLACIUS (1520-1575)

Born in Albona, today's Labin in Croatia close to Trieste, a region which in those times was Venetian territory, Flacius belongs to the second generation of Lutheran reformers. A controversial figure in the history and theology of the Reformation especially because of his criticism of Melanchthon's works, as Robert Kolb points out.[1] Flacius is nonetheless a key theologian at least as important for Protestant historiography as Melanchthon himself. It is important though to realize that, as a Croatian, or as a non-German, Flacius was marginalized for a rather long time and his theology acquired some degree of fame only in the past few decades. Wade Johnston even points out that Flacius was frequently considered an outsider during his lifetime and this aspect was often emphasized by his theological opponents.[2]

Like any other Lutheran theologian, Flacius wrote a lot about forensic justification about which he says that it is anchored in the foundation provided by Christ's work, and in this respect Christ's righteousness is imputed to the sinner by faith alone, not infused by grace. Regarding this particular aspect of Flacius's theology, Olli-Pekka Vainio writes that "Flacian terminology efficiently safeguarded faith against ideas of faith as an infused virtue."[3] Flacius intended to demonstrate that Lutheran theology continues Catholic theology; this is why Donald Kelley shows that Flacius always contended that the universality or catholicity of the church is based on *successio doctrinae*, the dogmatic succession of ecclesiastical teachings, not on the apostolic succession, because the dogmatic succession is a continuous chain of theological realities connected to the early church.[4]

Oliver Olson reveals that Flacius also attempted to prove the connection between Lutheranism and the Eastern Orthodox church which he commended because (1) it never accepted the pope's primacy, (2) it always rejected the doctrine of the purgatory, (3) it never embraced the private mass for the dead, (4) it never promoted indulgences, (5) it never accepted priestly celibacy, and (6) it never promoted the veneration of statues representing the saints, Mary, and Jesus.[5]

In trying to connect the Reformation to the previous ecclesiastical tradition of medieval Catholicism and patristic antiquity, Flacius managed rather successfully to identify a series of theologians who, during their ecclesiastical careers, not only foretold but also prepared the way for the doctrinal ideas promoted by Luther's reformation. Thus, according to Ronald Rittgers, Flacius reminded us that Johannes Tauler used to frequently mention that the human being must put his trust in God alone, while

---

1. Kolb, *Lutheran Ecclesiastical Culture, 1550–1675*, 36.
2. Johnston, *Devil behind the Surplice*, 62.
3. Vainio, *Justification and Participation in Christ*, 116.
4. Kelley, *Beginning of Ideology*, 121.
5. Olson, "Matthias Flacius," 88.

Lutheran Theology (2)

Hildegard von Bingen did not refrain from saying that the pope should be honored only for his spiritual accomplishments, not for his military actions that much too often turned into genuine wars in the wake of which countless numbers of Catholic believers lost their lives; the list, however, is longer and includes other famous names like Bernard de Clairvaux, Mechthild von Magdeburg, and Jean Gerson.[6]

Phillip Haberkern proves that, as a Lutheran, Flacius did not see any problem in vehemently criticizing the political power of the pope[7] and of the German princes, although his theological interests were eventually much more important than his political opinions. Thus, theologically speaking, Flacius was one of the first Lutheran theologians to become extremely preoccupied with modern hermeneutics, or the interpretation of sacred texts in a totally distinct manner from that provided by medieval Catholic schools influenced by rationalist scholasticism.

One of his most famous works is *Clavis scripturae sacrae* (The Key to the Holy Scripture), an extremely influential book in which Flacius lays the foundation of modern hermeneutics by establishing a set of fundamental rules for the interpretation of the Holy Scripture's texts. For instance, Deborah Shuger describes Flacius's *Clavis* as "an exhaustive treatment of biblical language in its philological, grammatical, and rhetorical aspects . . . a far more original and sophisticated study of religious language than any other sixteenth-century rhetoric."[8]

Concretely, in *Clavis*, Flacius convincingly argues that the Bible has only one meaning, and this is the universal meaning, namely the meaning intended by the author which is always preferable to its metaphorical counterpart. As far as Robert Christman is concerned, Flacius's *Clavis* deals with Scripture as a special book which presents Christ's work, an aspect never to be ignored in any hermeneutical endeavor because it can minimize the "role of Christ in salvation."[9]

Last but not least, and this aspect is powerfully underlined by Flacius, Scripture has a unique meaning because it speaks in one voice, and this voice permanently confesses Christ who did everything for us. This is precisely why Flacius criticizes Melanchthon; in fact, as Michael Mullett

---

6. Rittgers, *Reformation of Suffering*, 220.
7. Haberkern, *Patron Saint and Prophet*, 275.
8. Shuger, *Sacred Rhetoric*, 73.
9. Christman, *Doctrinal Controversy and Lay Religiosity in Late Reformation Germany*, 50.

tells us, Flacius rejects Melanchthon's synergism,[10] which he identifies as false since the human being does not cooperate with God regarding his justification. Repentance is not produced by the law, as Melanchthon seems to imply, but always by the gospel, as Flacius himself points out numerous times in his works:

> This righteousness of obedience is what God asks from us even after the fall and is therefore noble because it is with this that he convinces us about the fact that we have no righteousness before him. Therefore, it is reasonable and correct that we should be assigned to everlasting corruption and hellish condemnation. We need help to escape this situation, so we must seek him who worked for us the righteousness of obedience which we could have never reached otherwise.[11]

What ultimately matters for Flacius is God's initiative in saving the human being from his sinful situation. In this respect, he emphatically says that we cannot contribute anything to salvation; whatever we have and works for our salvation is not ours, but God's. As sinful beings in desperate need of salvation, what we do have is corruption and, hence, condemnation. There is no way in which we could have ever reached salvation had it not been for God's gracious initiative so wonderfully presented by Paul McGlasson as "a gracious and surprising event . . . never factored into . . . the ingredients of human nature."[12]

ARGULA VON GRUMBACH (1490–1564)

Argula is a special case because she was one of the relatively few women who promoted Luther's evangelical teachings not only in practice but also in writing. A lay person and mother of four children, Argula began her theological career as early as 1523 when a certain Arsacius Seehofer was severely tortured until he swore on the gospel that he was willing to give up his reformation ideas. According to Andrew Thomas, the only person who had the courage to publicly defend him was Argula.[13] This spectacle held obviously in public was organized by the University of Ingolstadt, the bulwark of Bavarian Catholicism, which counted among its most celebrated

10. Mullett, *Historical Dictionary of the Reformation and Counter-Reformation*, 212.
11. Flacius Illyricus, *Von der Gerechtigkeit wider Osiandrum*.
12. McGlasson, *Church Doctrine*, 3:63.
13. Thomas, *Apocalypse in Reformation Nuremberg*, 76.

professors none other than Johann von Eck, Luther's famous opponent at the Leipzig Disputation of 1519.

As a result of this cheap theatrical performance, Argula wrote a letter in which she sternly criticizes the measures enforced by the University of Ingolstadt and in doing so she challenges its Catholic professors to a disputation in Latin (not German), which was supposed to be held based exclusively on Scripture. Peter Matheson discloses that Argula and her family—her husband, Fritz, and her brother Marcellus, who studied at the very university of Ingolstadt—had to go through series of problems initiated against them by ecclesiastical authorities.[14]

Even though her contribution to the development of the evangelical Reformation in Germany was episodical and fragmentary, Argula was famous enough to have been commended by Luther himself who nonetheless never considered her an authentic theologian.[15] Deeply interested in Scripture and showing no propensity for philosophy, Argula uses many biblical quotations in her works because, as she herself contended, one must always search for the truth. Thus, being convinced that truth can be found only in Scripture, Brad Gregory attests that—according to Argula—the Holy Spirit gives wisdom through the Bible[16] and the theologian's duty is to find the truth of Scripture in prayer.

By reading Scripture, Christians realize that God calls them by name and the true theology all Christians must confess is the theology of God's word. Unlike the words of the human being, Argula shows that every word uttered by God in Scripture is true, so the Christian has the duty to live according to God's law revealed in Scripture's "genuine light."[17] This is vital for Christian life because unlike the world which is transient, God's word remains forever, and this perennial character is what turns Scripture into a genuine defense wall for ever believer.

In fact, as we can see in Stephen Murray, Argula points out that God's word is the shield of every Christian—but also "a rod, a murder weapon, to those who forsake it, resist it"[18]—because he is not able to live according to God's will unless he defends himself against sin by using the shield of God's word, the life-giving force which is never left fruitless. In this particular

14. Matheson, *Argula von Grumbach (1492–1554/7)*, 80–82.
15. Matheson, *Argula von Grumbach (1492–1554/7)*, 83.
16. Gregory, *Unintended Reformation*.
17. Taylor and Choi, *Handbook of Women Biblical Interpreters*.
18. Murray, *Reclaiming Divine Wrath*, 120.

context, Argula makes great use of the language and imagery of birth. God gives life, she writes, in the sense that he causes all of us to be born again through his Word. Also, Nathalie K. Watson shows how, in Argula's theology, "God's living word . . . generates life out of chaos."[19] God gives us life first through creation then by forgiving our sins through salvation, unlike the pope who squeezes life out of the church. One of Argula's favorite images is the fountain of life; God himself is the fountain of life and his "yes" leaves no room for "no."

This is why Argula presents God as the one who quenches our spiritual thirst through Christ, the only true light of all genuine believers. Thus, believers find all these things in Scripture which is God's gift to all those who live in humility. This gift of God is God's light for all human beings, although it remains concealed from those who live in the world as unrepented sinners. It is clear that Argula love Scripture and she did so from childhood when—as Ruth Tucker reminds us—at the age of ten, "her father had given her a gift of a beautifully illustrated Koberger Bible, a treasure that she repeatedly read and memorized."[20] Scripture is important for Argula, because, as her own words attest, Scripture reveals Christ himself:

> I beseech you, for God's sake, not to believe your own words all the time, but to check them against the Holy Scripture, as John says in his first epistle: he who is from God acknowledges Christ . . . It is not enough if we say: "I believe what my parents believed"; we must believe in God, not in (the beliefs of) our parents. When an adult person has the right faith . . . then Christ says: "The one who acknowledges me before men, I shall also acknowledge before my father, but that who does not acknowledge me, I cannot acknowledge either."[21]

The mystery of this reality unveils the apocalyptic character of Argula's theology which promotes the idea that through salvation God turns the world upside down and this is sufficient reason for all Christians to fight against the evil doers who hate the true light. In this regard, Sujin Pak explains that Argula used biblical texts like Matthew 24 and 25 to voice her apocalyptic convictions.[22] Since the Bible presents the battle between life and death, light and darkness, genuine Christians should always expect to

---

19. Watson, *Feminist Theology*, 6.
20. Tucker, *Extraordinary Women of Christian History*.
21. Von Grumbach, *Schriften*, 87–88.
22. Sujin Pak, *Reformation of Prophecy*, 58.

be threatened with death and even suffer death because of the gospel like Jesus (Argula herself received death threats following her criticism of what happened at the University of Ingolstadt as well as of the actions taken by its professors).

Argula issues some warnings of her own, also noticed by Roland Bainton: those who forbid Luther's theology, she believes, will be hit by various calamities like the pharaoh in the Old Testament, and if God's word is forgotten (see the pharaoh's case again), order and civilization will be wiped out from the face of the earth according to the pattern provided by diluvian history; but first and foremost, the political leaders, the princes, may suffer the fate of Pharaoh.[23] According to Argula, such a scenario is not beyond possibility, because wherever the word of God reigns unrestrained, the pope, the emperor, and all earthly rulers have no power whatsoever.

As far as Argula is concerned, the methods used by the inquisition turn the executioner into the world's best theologian because such a person destroys the theology of those who agree with these methods and resort to persecution. The gospel should be free circulate throughout the human society because God's word was entrusted to Christians in their capacity as members of society. Christians are not allowed to keep God's word only for themselves; on the contrary, they must preach it from the rooftops despite all difficulties, threats, and dangers of all sorts. Likewise, Christians must never be ashamed of Christ lest Christ should be ashamed of them. As Matheson proves, in Argula it is clear that all Christians must expect difficulties in life because the apprentice is never above his master.[24]

Since Christ suffered, Christians must also suffer and Luther's case is important in this respect, Argula contends. Luther, she believed, was hated by everybody like every Christian who loves Scripture. In fact, Christians are hated because of Scripture which, in its capacity as God's word, is like (1) the fire which destroys everything, (2) the sledgehammer which crushes stones, and (3) the storm which sweeps away everything on its path. This is why, Argula says, God's word will always cause those in the world to persecute Christians who must never hesitate to put their lives at risk for the sake of the gospel. However, as Derek Wilson claims, Argula never saw herself as a "lutheran," but rather as an "evangelical" and, in this sense, a follower and a confessor of Christ, not of Luther.[25]

23. Bainton, *Women of the Reformation in Germany and Italy*, 106.
24. Matheson, *Argula von Grumbach (1492–1554/7)*, 76.
25. Wilson, *Out of the Storm*.

Christians make up the church, and the church's most important sign is the correct preaching of God's word, like in Luther's theology, a reality which the clergy must always carry out despite all dangers. Thus, Christians must never worry about anything because God always avenges the sufferings of his servants, Argula believes. Christ, our rock,[26] will crush all our persecutors, she used to say, and God himself will turn people's curses into blessings for the elect.[27] The church has the power to live fearlessly because she is built on the foundation of God's word and the guidance of the Holy Spirit; thus, the church must make disciples and use all her spiritual gifts. The church is God's people,[28] in which capacity believers must confess Christ by words and deeds, so they must speak in Christ's name if they truly want to benefit from God's protection.

Argula was convinced that between the church and God there is a covenant which is based on the fact that God accepts us while we must also accept and confess him before all people. She also approves of the priesthood of believers because Christians, who make up the church, are God's children so they behave like the sheep that recognize the voice of the shepherd. All Christians are equal because they share the same baptism and must live in such a way that they fulfill their obligations and responsibilities while not taking advantage of the rights given by the gospel. As Matheson indicates, in Argula, the church is served by pastors and doctors (teachers) who are not priests, but servants of God and of the church's head, Jesus Christ, who reveals to us that the only guide of the church is Scripture.[29]

All Christians have the duty and obligation to serve God by making full use of the Holy Scripture to preach the gospel in society. Thus, the church has a prophetic (homiletical) role because of the constant support provided by the Holy Spirit who is not only the true teacher of the church, but also the one helping her to spread the gospel everywhere. Christina Moss and Gary Waite confirm that, in Argula, all people—peasants and women, those of low social status and those in high political places—are "beneficiaries of the Holy Spirit."[30] Christians cannot do anything without the Holy Spirit; they are all weak and all they can do is sin, but the Spirit

---

26. Matheson, *Argula von Grumbach (1492–1554/7)*, 73.

27. Selderhuis, *Psalms 73–150*, 357.

28. Matheson, *Argula von Grumbach (1492–1554/7)*, 63.

29. Matheson, "Argula von Grumbach," 102.

30. Moss and Waite, "Argula von Grumbach, Katharina Schütz Zell, and Anabaptist and Jorist Women," 164.

Lutheran Theology (2)

gives them strength, unites them with God, and transforms them internally as well as spiritually. Even if she does not mention justification by faith alone, the classical trinitarian formulae, or the dialectics between law and gospel, Argula provides us with a practical theology which actively supported the consolidation and the dissemination of early Lutheran theology[31] across the entire land of Germany, especially among simple folk.

ASSESSMENT QUESTIONS

1. How does Flacius explain the continuity between Lutheran theology and Catholic theology?
2. How does Flacius explain the resemblances between Lutheran theology and Eastern Orthodox theology?
3. What is the essence of modern hermeneutics as promoted by Flacius?
4. What does Argula von Grumbach say about Scripture and is role?
5. How does Argula von Grumbach explain the duty of Christians towards God?

---

31. Cameron, *European Reformation*, 231.

5

Lutheran Theology (3)
Urbanus Rhegius, Johannes Brenz, and Martin Chemnitz

OBJECTIVES

1. To comprehend the main aspects of Rhegius's theology;
2. To recognize the main aspects of Brenz's theology;
3. To be aware of the main aspects of Chemnitz's theology;
4. To be acquainted with Brenz's political philosophy and theology;
5. To learn the Lutheran reaction against Catholic theology.

Key words: Rhegius, Brenz, Chemnitz, justification, assurance, state

URBANUS RHEGIUS (1489-1541)

Rhegius was preoccupied with pastoral theology even before he became a reformer, so his interest in pastoral care marked his entire career since he was still a Catholic, during which time he had focused intensely on the teaching and education of priests. Margaret Arnold informs us that he even wrote a preaching manual aimed at educating evangelical ministers.[1]

---

1. Arnold, *Magdalene in the Reformation*.

Lutheran Theology (3)

Following his decision to join Luther, Rhegius starts to criticize indulgences[2] by saying that the only true indulgence is God's grace based on the cross of Christ, an indulgence which must be received by faith alone, not by good works or by partaking into the sacraments.

Within the context of pastoral care, Rhegius attempts to develop a theology of the Lord's Supper which must be received exclusively by faith and thus be, as Scott Hendrix mentions, in line with the "roots of the early church."[3] The Lord's Supper is not a continuous sacrificing of Christ as in Catholic theology because eating Christ's body and drinking Christ's blood is nothing else but to have faith. In Rhegius's thought, the Lord's Supper presupposes, as far as the believer is concerned, thankfulness and gratitude for Christ's sacrifice on the cross, which has the power to forgive sins and to strengthen the believer in faith. On the other hand, faith is the only aspect which is capable of transforming the Lord's supper into an effective reality for the believer because, as we read in Lee Palmer Wandel, for Rhegius "the meal was a sign of God's promise."[4]

Rhegius worked closely with Melanchthon to draft a document which was intended to achieve a possible reconciliation with the Catholics since they both agreed, as admitted by Ragnar Andersen, on a range of issues specific to Catholic dogma.[5] According to this document, Catholics had to alter their theology in some respects, so they needed (1) to preach the true gospel without denying Christ, (2) to allow priests and monks to get married, and (3) to administer the Lord's Supper according to the Lutheran way, namely not only with bread but also with wine. All these issues were necessary, Rhegius believed, because they were clearly explained in Scripture and Scripture must always be received by faith alone. Arnold Snyder writes that, in Rhegius, whatever Scripture says, even about sensitive issues like political government, must be received with the same degree of faith, which is an extension and an exaggeration of "the role of government as described in Romans 13:1–5."[6]

This is why, in Rhegius's thought, the essence of Reformation theology is justification by faith alone, which must be evident not only in pastoral

---

2. Stewart, *Before Bruegel*, 70.
3. Hendrix, "Use of Scripture in Establishing Protestantism," 46.
4. Wandel, *Eucharist in the Reformation*, 62.
5. Andersen, *Concordia Ecclesiae*, 193–94.
6. Snyder, *Faith and Toleration*, 50.

care, but also in an obvious preoccupation for Christian missions, which begin with one's neighbor:

> Faith in Christ must begin when man believes that our sins are forgiven freely, only for the sake of Christ, our sole Mediator, through whom and for whose sake we have free entry to the Father and everything good is given to us for our use. Be warned, however, that the Lord Christ does not say in this (the Lord's) prayer that our sins will be forgiven so that we forgive those who sinned against us. Because we were not able to forgive our neighbors when we were still unbelievers; nevertheless, the Father has already forgiven our guilt for the sake of Christ. This is why our forgiveness is a seal and a secure landmark through which we are reminded that our own debts are forgiven.[7]

According to Rhegius, the Evangelical mission must be performed in two distinct stages: (1) taking the gospel to the regions where nobody knows about it and (2) preparing competent pastors who are supposed to be very well trained in the knowledge of Scripture as demonstrated by their own lives. Rhegius's works abound in references to faith, which must necessarily be accompanied by repentance and good works. Thus, Scott Hendrix reminds us that, in Rhegius, faith leads to repentance, and repentance to the forgiveness of sins; this is why the focus should always be on "preaching both repentance and faith."[8] Justification by faith alone does not imply avoiding good works; on the contrary, good works is a demonstration of justification and these truths about faith and repentance must be preached by all pastors.

JOHANNES BRENZ (1499–1570)

A reformer with an extremely rich activity, Brenz preached the gospel in the city of Stuttgart where he worked alongside his 13 children from two marriages. Horst Althaus reveals a very interesting aspect of Brenz's lineage, namely that among Brenz's direct descendants one should include Georg W. F. Hegel, the famous idealist philosopher,[9] while Hermann Ehmer includes another two equally famous names: Dietrich Bonhoeffer, the celebrated

---

7. Uhlhorn and Rhegius, *Urbanus Rhegius*, 231.
8. Hendrix, "Use of Scripture in Establishing Protestantism," 48.
9. Althaus, *Hegel*, 1.

Lutheran Theology (3)

Lutheran pastor executed by the Nazis, and Richard von Weitzsäcker, the former president of the German Federal Republic.[10]

One of the main focuses of Brenz's theology is God's word which caused him to accept the idea that the human being depends totally on God for his own salvation. In fact, Brenz used to point out, the human being depends exclusively on God's grace, on God's benevolence as the one who created him and can save him; and that is because, as we see in Richard Cross, due to Christ's dual nature "God dwells in Christ and in other human being."[11] Thus, the human being's salvation is based on God's grace which he can receive only by hearing God's word. Craig Farmer points out that, in Brenz, grace is a reality which originates in Christ who received it from the Father in the first place.[12] According to Brenz, God's word is identical with the very person of Christ and actively works the salvation of all human beings.

Salvation cannot become a reality for human beings unless God's word is preached, Brenz explains, because God's word alone can mediate the forgiveness of sins and justification, since both are received by the believer by faith alone. Brian Spinks notes that, in Brenz, "faith alone justifies,"[13] the core teaching of the Reformation. Christ and his spiritual gifts can be accepted only by faith, as demonstrated by the participation of the believer in the Lord's Supper which is the active presence of the gift of salvation, not only a symbol of brotherly communion. Christ, Brenz insists, is present in the elements of the Lord's Supper, in bread and wine, and his presence is real and physical because Christ's human nature shares the same features with his divine nature, so—as Joar Haga also mentions—Christ is ubiquitous or omnipresent.[14]

Christology is vital for Brenz's theology who identifies two essential aspects of the doctrine of Christ: (1) Jesus's salvific work and (2) the incarnation of the Word as a way to ransom humankind. The ransom is totally dependent on faith in Christ because Christ is in a perfect communion with God the Father. Christ is God and man; his divinity and humanity have an equal share (according to the patristic model of *communication idiomata*) in achieving the salvation of the sinful human being. Brenz was convinced

---

10. Ehmer, "Johannes Brenz (1499–1570)," 131.
11. Cross, *Communicatio Idiomatum*, 114.
12. Farmer, *Gospel of John in the Sixteenth Century*, 133.
13. Spinks, *Reformation and Modern Rituals and Theologies of Baptism*, 18.
14. Haga, *Was There a Lutheran Metaphysics?*, 137.

that man would have not been able to escape sin and death unless Jesus had been simultaneously both God and man, as Wolfhart Pannenberg writes, "from his birth onward."[15]

This is why, Brenz writes that God actively participates in Christ's suffering on the cross, and these achieve not only the salvation of every human being but also influence the life of every believer who received them by faith alone. Since every believer lives in society and is involved in its wellbeing, Ehmer believes that Brenz was deeply interested in providing a political philosophy.[16] The state, Brenz believed, was founded by God to prevent the spread of chaos in the world as a result of sin; so the foremost duty of the state is to promote peace and common good because maintaining peace is a divine command.

In Brenz's opinion, the state is the instrument of God's will, in which capacity it is responsible to supervise the enactment of God's commands for the good of all citizens. As for the citizens, they all have the duty to be subject to the state, so any revolt against the state is revolt against God who not only established the very existence of the state itself but also regulated all the duties of the state. As far as Steinmetz is concerned, in doing so Brenz "went beyond Luther in giving the state a role in the internal affairs of the church."[17] The only weapon the Christian is allowed to use against the state and its unjust actions is prayer; in more concrete terms, prayer which must be wielded daily, with passion and consistency, by all believers, including the pastors as spiritual leaders of ecclesiastical communities.

Thus, Brenz explains that the pastor has not only the right but also the obligation to criticize the policy of the state because there must be a harmony between God's word and law, religious or secular. The pastor, however, as well as all human beings must never focus on the law, but on the gospel and Christ:

> Man must not pursue the law but the Gospel. But as in past times, according to the law—which aimed at sin and unrighteous works—the calamity of sin results in punishment, now according to the gospel or Christ—which does not aim at sin . . . but at faith, the adversity is sent to us from God not as punishment for sin, as in the law, but as a cross. Because since Christ came, he rejected the sin of believers; he washed and cleansed them in his blood. So

---

15. Pannenberg, *Jesus God and Man*.
16. Ehmer, "Johannes Brenz (1499–1570)," 133.
17. Steinmetz, *Reformers in the Wings*, 78.

God ascribed to the cross no other meaning which is imposed on the believer than that he gave to his son, Jesus Christ.[18]

But the law, religious and secular, is here to stay. According to Brenz, the purpose of penal law is not to punish crimes (which is exclusively God's prerogative), but to intimidate those who want to commit crimes. The punishment of crimes must be done based on the Christian principles of mercy, benevolence, and justice, which must be present in the church as well. In this respect, Pietro Delcorno points to the fact that Brenz's use of the parable of the prodigal son "disavowed the need for a detailed confession," so "the confession became a *confessio fidei* instead of a *confessio peccatorum*."[19] Brenz insists that all these issues can be found in Scripture, so biblical theology must be a constant presence in the preaching of God's word as explained in catechisms which must be appropriated by all believers for a better knowledge of the essential teachings of the Christian faith.

Brenz's activity was extremely prolific as he preached almost every day, wrote commentaries on almost all the books of the Bible, and supported the dissemination of Protestantism in Germany through the reformation of the University of Tübingen and the establishment of its Faculty of Evangelical or Protestant Theology.[20] Beth Kreitzer shows that another critically important aspect of Brenz's reforming activity was his active participation in the drafting of marriage legal provisions in the duchy of Württemberg.[21] This was a vital aspect for the actual change of social mentalities and economic realities not only in the Bavarian land but also in the whole of Germany and ultimately in all the European countries which adhered to the teachings of the Protestant Reformation

MARTIN CHEMNITZ (1522–1586)

A reformer of the second generation and one of Melanchthon's students,[22] Chemnitz founded his entire theology on the distinction between the law and the gospel which he applied to all Protestant doctrines. This aspect was crucial for Chemnitz because, as Quentin Steward demonstrates, his use

---

18. Brenz, *Etlich Tractetli*.
19. Delcorno, *In the Mirror of the Prodigal Son*, 399.
20. Ehmer, "Johannes Brenz (1499–1570)," 128.
21. Kreitzer, *Reforming Mary*, 100.
22. Vainio, *Justification and Participation in Christ*, 119.

of the law and the gospel was part of his doctrine of justification.[23] Thus, Chemnitz criticized Andreas Osiander's doctrine of ontological justification by pointing out that Christ's divine righteousness does not become united with the believer, but always remains an external reality to him. Within the context of justification, Chemnitz explains that one can never speak about the ontological transfer of Christ's righteousness upon the believer because Christ's righteousness is transferred upon the believer only forensically and declaratively, namely by imputation, not ontologically. In Brenz's spiritual equation, this reality, according to Anthony Lane, turns believers into God's adopted children and beneficiaries of eternal life.[24]

This reality must reflect itself on the doctrine of the Lord's Supper, according to which—as Richard Cross informs us[25]—Christ's body and blood are present in a real way in the bread and wine of the Lord's Supper. Thus, the bread and wine (with Christ's body and blood) must be received both by believers and unbelievers, Chemnitz opines, because Christ's righteousness is forensically transferred upon all those who trust him. Since Chemnitz was a staunch defender of Christ's real and substantial presence in the eucharistic elements, Bryan Spinks thinks that participating at the Lord's Supper is a divine blessing.[26] Nevertheless, trust, which is the essence of faith, must be activated in unbelievers and constantly reactivated in believers so that all should be partakers of Christ's presence.

Jack Kilcrease notices that in Chemnitz's thought, Christ is simultaneously God and human,[27] while his divinity and humanity work together for the salvation of believers based on the patristic principle of *communicatio idiomata*. Thus, as part of his person, Christ's divine and human natures are present not only in the Lord's Supper but also in his incarnation; as for incarnation, the union of divinity and humanity in Christ's person, allowed the savior to perform two actions which would be otherwise impossible to any human being: (1) to die for sins (because he is both God and man) and (2) to be exalted to the right hand of the Father (because he is both God and man). This is how Chemnitz explains God's decision to deal with human sin in Christ:

23. Stewart, *Lutheran Patristic Catholicity*, 89.
24. Lane, *Regensburg Article 5 on Justification*, 127.
25. Cross, *Communicatio Idiomatum*, 187.
26. Spinks, *Do This in Remembrance of Me*, 261.
27. Kilcrease, *Self-Donation of God*, 156.

> It is proper, therefore, for God to cleanse and destroy sin . . . , but Scripture clearly attributes this action not only to the person of the incarnate Christ according to the deity, but also to His blood according to the humanity. And we must not understand this only as a matter of merit when His blood was poured out on the cross, but it is also to be understood as a matter of efficacy and application; for Scripture attributes our very justification and the reconciliation of the sinner with God to this blood. For the statement in 1 John 1:9 concerning the person, that He is faithful and just to cleanse us from all unrighteousness.[28]

Chemnitz unequivocally criticized the theology of the Council of Trent by defending the inspiration of Scripture which he describes as God's word. Moreover, Chemnitz defends the sufficiency and clarity of Scripture by pointing out that the Bible contains all the things God wants us to know about him and his will. Truth about God can be found only through the eyes of faith since the human being is considered righteous and innocent before God only by the imputation of Christ's righteousness which is received by faith alone, not by one's merits or good works.[29]

In Chemnitz's theology, as showed by Robert Kolb, the foundation of salvation is Christ's suffering for the forgiveness of sins based on which God's word, namely Jesus Christ, justifies us or considers us righteous as God's act of re-creation.[30] In other words, through justification, God creates as again, for the second time. Justification is the second creation of the human being by God and whoever wants to have it must receive it by faith alone. Thus, according to Chemnitz, faith is the instrument which helps us search for, appropriate, receive, and live the word of God's gospel. Through justification, the human being partakes in God's mercy which forgives and eradicates sins as well as accepts us into eternal life for the sake of Jesus Christ, described by Brenz—and we see this in Vainio—as God's son and our mediator.[31]

Gottfried Martens reminds us that Chemnitz wrote consistently about faith which he defines as trust (*fiducia*) in God.[32] Faith is a gift in which capacity it is offered by God to all believers who must be aware that faith cannot be acquired by one's own efforts. The actions of the human being

---

28. Chemnitz, *Two Natures in Christ*, 330.
29. Jackson, *Catholic, Lutheran, Protestant*, 120.
30. Kolb, "Human Performance and the Righteousness of Faith," 133.
31. Vainio, *Justification and Participation in Christ*, 151.
32. Martens, *Die Rechtfertigung des Sünders*, 102.

can never lead to faith; only God himself can initiate a connection with human beings through the mediation of faith which he himself offers as gift. Thus, only God is the initiator and supporter of salvation which begins with justification and is achieved (1) by grace alone, (2) without payment (*gratis*), (3) without the law, (4) without (good) works, (5) by the imputation of Christ's righteousness, and (6) by the forgiveness of sins. But, as Robert Koons writes, in Chemnitz's theology, faith works in love, so God's gift of salvation through faith must result in good works.[33]

Thus, in Chemnitz, good works are the necessary result of faith as a gift offered by God. According to David Scaer's interpretation of Chemnitz, good works must demonstrate justification, but they contribute nothing to the actual achievement of justification because James's "to be justified" is nothing but Paul's "to be considered justified."[34] Likewise, good works prove that justification can be appropriated exclusively by faith alone, which is received from God himself. Within this particular context, Chemnitz mentions election, which he defines as an expression of Jesus Christ's gospel. Richard Lenski even points out that, in Chemnitz, election was important enough to end up in his sermons.[35] Consequently, predestination for eternal condemnation is impossible and believers should never worry about their election.

According to Scripture, Chemnitz points out, every believer is deeply assured of his own salvation, which is confirmed by God's grace, by the promise of the gospel that forgives sins, by baptism, and by the Lord's Supper. Anthony Lane correctly notices that Chemnitz's argument in favor of election is based on Christ's external righteousness, not on our inherent righteousness.[36] Chemnitz, therefore, is convinced that every believer must trust the words of Scripture which promises that nothing can separate him from the love of God in Christ, and if God himself promises to take care of the believer, then this will happen for sure, as the apostle Paul plainly explains in his *Epistle to the Romans* (8:28–39). In the end, as Steven Paulson writes about Chemnitz's theology, it is pastorally crucial to see God as "having mercy on whom he will" for our own comfort.[37]

---

33. Koons, *Lutheran's Case for Roman Catholicism*, 3.
34. Scaer, *James, the Apostle of Faith*, 140.
35. Lenski, *Interpretation of St. Matthew's Gospel, Chapters 15–28*, 859.
36. Lane, *Justification by Faith in Catholic-Protestant Dialogue*, 212.
37. Paulson, *Lutheran Theology*, 218.

ASSESSMENT QUESTIONS

1. What provisions were included in the agreement with Catholics which Rhegius drafted with Melanchthon?
2. What are the main aspects of Brenz's christology?
3. What does Brenz say about the state in his political philosophy?
4. How does Chemnitz criticize the doctrine of justification in Osiander's theology?
5. What does Chemnitz have to say about justification, good works, and the assurance of salvation?

6

Reformed Theology (1)
Ulrich Zwingli and Heinrich Bullinger

OBJECTIVES

1. To understand the relationship between Christ and salvation in Zwingli's theology;
2. To know the connection between the Spirit and the word in Zwingli's theology;
3. To comprehend Zwingli's theology of the sacraments;
4. To recognize Bullinger's theology of God's election;
5. To become familiar with Bullinger's theology of justification and sanctification.

Key words: Zwingli, Bullinger, sovereignty, election, justification, grace

ULRICH ZWINGLI (1484–1531)

Like Luther, Zwingli was brought up to become a Catholic theologian under the powerful influence of medieval scholastic theology and humanist philosophy. The Reformation initiated by Zwingli in Zürich was different from Luther's Reformation in Wittenberg especially with reference to two fundamental doctrines: God's providence and the Lord's Supper. According to Gottfried Locher, in Zwingli, providence "does not compete with

Reformed Theology (1)

faith in Christ, but rather constitutes the consequence and proof of that faith,"[1] while the Lord's Supper expresses, as we are told by Bruce Gordon, his "vision of the Christian community."[2] Thus, one of the basic features of Zwingli's theology is the priority of the doctrine of God which was one of his main preoccupations since as early as 1516 when, under the influence of humanism, Zwingli decides to give up medieval scholastic theology and philosophy in order to focus his entire attention on the study of Scripture in its original languages: Hebrew and Greek.

Johann Kurtz tells us that, in 1522, Zwingli decided firmly to reject the authority of the pope and of church hierarchy,[3] so in taking this step he placed himself within the Evangelical Reformation movement initiated by Luther although, according to his own confession, he did the Zürich Reformation without any prior knowledge of what had happened in Wittenberg. In those years, Zwingli was busy studying the relationship between Christ and salvation which became the main characteristic of its theology after 1522. This powerful christological overtone prompted him to conclude, like Oscar Pfister, that forgiveness of sins is not dependent on bishops and priests or on meritorious works, but on Christ alone who sacrificed himself for humankind.[4] In Zwingli's words:

> God alone remits sin through Jesus Christ, his Son, and alone our Lord. Who assigns this to creatures detracts from the honor of God and gives it to him who is not God; this is idolatry. Hence the confession which is made to the priest or neighbor shall not be declared to be a remittance of sin, but only a seeking for advice. Works of penance coming from the counsel of human beings ... do not cancel sin; they are imposed as a menace to others. Christ has borne all our pains and labor. Hence whoever assigns to works of penance what belongs to Christ errs and slanders God.[5]

Assiduously searching Scripture, Zwingli realizes that Jesus Christ did everything for the salvation of men and women, so these must now seek help in Christ, not in other people who are merely created beings. K. J. Drake confirms that Zwingli was interested both in the humanity and the divinity

---

1. Locher, *Zwingli's Thought*, 166.
2. Gordon, *Zwingli*, 136.
3. Kurtz, *Church History*, 2:264.
4. Pfister, *Christianity and Fear*.
5. Zwingli, *Ulrich Zwingli (1484–1931)*.

of Christ[6] although, in his writings, the weight is placed almost invariably on Christ's divine nature which forces him to admit that Jesus Christ ransomed us from sin and forgives us our sins precisely because he is God. This explains Zwingli's decision, as Hubert Cunliffe-Jones suggests, "to link salvation more closely to God's sovereign election."[7]

It is clear then why the human being must place his entire trust in Christ as God, as he himself did.[8] Christ's humanity must not be ignored either because it is because of his humanity that Christ is a model of morality, an ethical example for all Christians who are bound to follow it if they truly wish to enjoy God's salvation whose absolute sovereignty Zwingli affirms without reservation or equivocation. Thus—as also shown by Locher—he believes that all things belong to God's providence[9] and nothing in the entire creation happens without God's will and command; nothing in the whole universe happens without God knowing.

According to Zwingli, there is a connection between the human being and God although any comparison between the human being and God is nearly impossible because the human being is like clay in the potter's hands, as Zwingli was ready to admit in 1519 when—we find from Jennifer Awes Freeman—he barely made it alive following some long weeks of illness caused by the plague.[10] It is God alone who gives us life and takes it away, although the vividly real character of God's sovereignty must never lead to resignation; on the contrary, it must lead to active involvement in the life of the church. The human being has the duty to subject himself to God with all his trust and faith.

In Zwingli's thought, salvation comes exclusively from God through Christ as a result of God's free choice; it is God's decision who is saved and who is not, without any human being's actual knowledge of God. Pan-Chiu Lai competently proves that this is a demonstration of God's absolute sovereignty, Zwingli insisted, because God is free to choose whoever he pleases for salvation, including ancient pagan philosophers like Socrates, whom Zwingli was convinced would meet in heaven.[11] The Holy Spirit is free to draw whomever he wishes to himself because salvation does not depend on

---

6. Drake, *Flesh of the Word*, 71.
7. Cunliffe-Jones, *A History of Christian Doctrine*, 362.
8. Bahrych, *Practical Disciplines of a Christian Life*.
9. Locher, *Zwingli's Thought*, 166.
10. Awes Freeman, "'And Who Is My Neighbor?,'" 75.
11. Lai, *Towards a Trinitarian Theology of Religions*, 40.

external means such as the sacraments, the church, Scripture or even the knowledge of Christ, but on God's free choice alone.

Another feature of Zwingli's theology is the relationship between the Holy Spirit and God's word. The Spirit cannot be restricted to Scripture and sacraments, because he works according to his own will in full accordance with God's will. On the other hand, Isaak August Dorner points out that, in Zwingli, the word is twofold: (1) external (Scripture listened to without the Spirit) and (2) internal (Scripture obeyed in full and understood with the Spirit's assistance).[12] Every Christian is bound to read the Scriptures and thus be a *God-taught* person, somebody who learns on his own about God from Scripture and relies on nobody else for this.

The internal word validates itself by offering us existential security, which means that the anointing of the Spirit frees us from the necessity of a human teacher. This is why Zwingli appears to ascribe more importance to the Spirit than to the word, an aspect which was not only noticed but also severely criticized by Luther. Zwingli, however, did not separate the Spirit from the word; in fact, he explained that it its capacity as written word, Scripture talks about the incarnate Word, Jesus Christ. According to Malcolm Yarnell, in Zwingli's theology, the relationship between the written word (Scripture) and the incarnate Word (Christ) can be understood only through the help provided by the Holy Spirit.[13]

As he studied Scripture very early each morning alongside his students, Zwingli concluded that even if allegory may be permitted, Scripture has only one true and natural meaning which deciphers the mysteries of the written word. Based on this conviction, Zwingli began a thorough study of the then highly controversial theology of the sacraments which he approached from the standpoint of justification by faith alone conceived, as we can see in Mark Thompson, as reconciliation to God.[14] Drawing on the Augustinian definition of the sacrament, Zwingli insists that this is the sign of a holy reality. Thus, Wayne Baker reveals that, in Zwingli, "the sacrament functions as the external sealing of an inner, invisible work."[15] This means that the sacrament has two aspects: internal and external, although the administration of the sacrament (which is an external sign) causes no spiritual change within the person who receives it (which is an internal sign).

---

12. Dorner, *History of Protestant Theology*, 1:297.
13. Yarnell, "Person and Work of the Holy Spirit," 513.
14. Thompson, *Celebrating the Reformation*.
15. Baker, "Zwingli, Huldrych (1484–1531)," 899.

In other words, the sacrament does not causally determine the meaning of the thing which he points to, but only confirms its existence. The sacrament is a sign of grace, Zwingli says, not an instrument of grace, so the sacrament talks about divine grace without offering it to us. Grace can be received only by faith, and this needs no signs or sacraments; this is why salvation, achieved in and through Christ, cannot be limited to sacraments, very much like it cannot be limited to the people of Israel. Last but not least, John Rempel insists that "Zwingli's emphasis in his teaching on the sacraments . . . was on the divine will,"[16] so the sacraments offer no guarantee to anyone as they are effective only due to the Holy Spirit's divine will.

In Zwingli's theology, infant baptism is valid because it continues the theology of the covenant between God and the human being as presented in the Old Testament; infant baptism though does not save but only illustrates the placing of the child under a covenant validated by God himself for all human beings—in the words of John Wheelan Riggs, "infant baptism was . . . a pledge sign . . . since it was the parallel to circumcision by which the children of Abraham were to be raised in the covenant."[17] The Lord's Supper is only an event which reminds us of Christ's sacrifice; Christ is not present in a real way in bread and wine because he is present physically in heaven, at the Father's right hand. Thus, Jan Jongeneel is convinced that, in Zwingli, Christ's presence at the Lord's Supper is only symbolic and spiritual.[18]

Those who partake in the Lord's Supper are God's true believers; the Lord's Supper is effective only for them anyway since they are the true church, not the ecclesiastical hierarchy of the Roman church. Richard Kyle makes an important point regarding Zwingli's eucharistic theology, based on his symbolic interpretation of the words of institution which shifted the weight of the eucharistic event from Christ's presence in the consecrated elements to the believer's presence in the gathering of the church: "He regarded the Lord's supper as a memorial (thankful recollection), a pledge (the reassurance of faith), and a public confession (union with the church)."[19]

In Zwingli's theology, the true church exists wherever the word and the Spirit are present, namely wherever Christ is proclaimed by preaching

16. Rempel, *Lord's Supper in Anabaptism*, 44.
17. Riggs, *Baptism in the Reformed Tradition*, 24.
18. Jongeneel, *Jesus Christ in World History*, 182.
19. Kyle, *God's Watchman*, 143.

and people decide to live for Christ by searching the Scriptures and applying all its teachings which are interpreted spiritually by the Holy Spirit. Consequently, church ministers must be fully prepared biblically, so they must know the Holy Scriptures as well as possible. Every preacher has the obligation as well as the duty to present God's will to all people and this can be done exclusively by searching and preaching the Holy Scriptures. Moreover, as Jacques Courvoisier tells us, not only the preachers, but also "all those who are members of the true church confess Jesus Christ without exception."[20]

HEINRICH BULLINGER (1504-1575)

Leader of the Zürich church after Zwingli's death in 1531,[21] Bullinger was never a systematician or a biblical theologian; all he wanted to do was to practically apply the teachings of Scripture. Bullinger was always convinced that he was merely a preacher, a pastor whose duty is to bring God's word among the people because, as we see in David Brown, it was Bullinger's conviction that "both the written Scripture and oral proclamation are brought together through the Holy Spirit."[22] Extremely preoccupied with the church and its fate, this was and will remain forever the central aspect of Bullinger's life and activity, who anchored his reformation efforts on the careful study of the Holy Scriptures.

As far as the Scriptures were concerned, Bullinger believed that they must be deciphered first; this is the foremost task of every theologian because, as Henk van den Belt mentions, in Bullinger's theology "scripture has its authority from itself."[23] Scripture must be searched and studied exegetically, since the purpose of exegesis is always to achieve clarity and simplicity. Bullinger was convinced that the biblical message must never be adorned with complex interpretations, so the preacher must always be sensitive about the rhetorical nature of God's word which can be understood by everybody as it unveils God's very nature. Through Scripture, Bullinger insists, God reveals his true nature to all human beings. God's nature is the creative and supporting force of all things and all beings. Scripture teaches us that God has a close relationship with the created world as demonstrated

---

20. Courvoisier, *Zwingli*, 55.
21. Moots, *Politics Reformed*, 35.
22. Brown, *Transformational Preaching*, 284.
23. Van den Belt, *Authority of Scripture in Reformed Theology*, 92.

by the covenant of grace. In this respect, John von Rohr believes that, in Bullinger, the covenant of grace "was a conditional covenant" because it explains the relationship between God and his creation.[24]

Mark Karlberg shows how, according to Bullinger, the covenant of grace unveils the nature of salvation throughout human history and the lives of the elect.[25] People benefit from the covenant of grace because grace does not depend on the human being's response, but on God's goodness and love. Following in Zwingli's footsteps, Bullinger explains that grace, grace alone can offer justification to the human being. The covenant of grace has two provisions: (1) God sent Christ for the salvation of human beings from sin and punishment and (2) Human beings must accept God's laws in obedience. The central aspect of this covenant is Christ who, in his capacity as God and man, fulfills God's providence in the history of humankind, hence—as Barbara Pitkin points out—'stressing the continuity of God's covenant of grace and one church of Christ through the ages."[26]

Because he has two natures, divine and human, Christ can achieve salvation on behalf of human beings due to God's grace and benevolence which—as Edward Dewey informs us—is manifested through this covenant of grace and God's promise.[27] God's intervention in the created world, however, has a specific purpose, that of solving the problem of human sin. Sin, however, is not the result of God's actions; Bullinger is convinced that God is not the author of sin and evil, but the human being. In his providence, God only allows the existence of evil and sin according to his sovereign will which works according to his divine plans by tuning evil into good according to God's goodness. Here is Bullinger's explanation:

> the providence of God does not disturb the order of things; it does not abrogate the offices of life, nor our labor and industry; it does not take [away] a just dispensation and obedience. But by these things, it works the health of those men who, through the help of God, religiously apply themselves to the decrees, purpose, or working of the Lord. They rightly ascribe to these whatever good happens to them; imputing to man's corruption, to our own unskillfulness, and to our sins, whatever evil happens to us. Therefore, the saints acknowledge that, by God's providence, wars, plagues, and diverse other calamities afflict mortal men; yet

24. Von Rohr, *Covenant of Grace in Puritan Thought*, 193.
25. Karlberg, *Covenant Theology in the Reformed Perspective*, 22.
26. Pitkin, *Calvin, the Bible, and History*, 28.
27. Dowey, "Heinrich Bullinger as Theologian," 55.

notwithstanding, the causes of these arise from nothing else than the sins of man. For God is good, who wishes us good rather than evil. Indeed, oftentimes of his goodness, he turns our evil purposes to good ends, as seen by the history of Joseph in the book of Genesis.[28]

Thus, God decides to elect and then actually elects all those who are going to be saved, although nobody can say for sure that God also elects those who will be condemned to eternal death. On the other hand, Bullinger believes that, based on the Scriptures, it is certain that even those who will go through eternal death will have been guilty of sins they had never repented of. The problem of sin is extremely serious for Bullinger because, as Robert Kolb tells us, sin has serious consequences in people's lives.[29] The fact that the saved had been previously elected by God is a testimony of God's mercy who demonstrates that he loves human beings and wishes the salvation of all. This is why the gospel must be preached to everybody; all human beings must hear the saving message because nobody knows who was or was not elected by God for salvation, but believers do share in what Moots calls "the spiritual legacy of Abraham's descendants."[30]

As far as we can tell as human beings, salvation is received based on faith which leads to justification and then sanctifies those who trust God. By faith alone, Christ becomes present in the believer while the latter begins to live for Christ alone and his righteousness which is counted as ours; John Fesko therefore writes that, according to Bullinger, "the believer is perfect because of the imputed righteousness of Christ."[31] Faith is sanctifying in Bullinger's theology because God can live within the human being only by faith after men and women have been born again spiritually. Faith is thus the human being's new birth through the transformation of his heart and mind which makes this infusion of Christ possible in the life of the believer. Judith Pollmann notices that, in Bullinger, the new birth is an epistemological landmark between a time when the believer did not know God and, of course, a subsequent time when he did.[32]

For Bullinger, justification by which the believer is considered innocent despite his sins is, in very real terms, his adoption by God. Fesko

28. Bullinger, *Decades of Henry Bullinger*, 578.
29. Kolb, "Human Nature, the Fall, and the Will," 26.
30. Moots, *Politics Reformed*, 45.
31. Fesko, *Beyond Calvin*, 181.
32. Pollmann, "Different Road to God," 55.

notices this connection between justification and adoption in Bullinger when he writes that "adoption is considered a forensic act, so Bullinger's inclusion of adoption under justification merely reflects the coordination of these two forensic benefits."[33] This way, justification is the beginning of a life-long process of sanctification. Justification does not automatically produce a perfect life but does initiate this process of growth into sanctification and holiness. It is through justification and sanctification that God lives in the very being of the born-again believer for the restoration of God's image within him. Pierrick Hildebrand is convinced that "Bullinger's reference to the restored *imago Dei* as a way of explaining what the original *imago Dei* was mean to be" means that "the possibility is left open for some glorified fulfillment achievable by unfallen man"[34]—in other words, a full restoration of God's image is possible only eschatologically.

As soon as the restoration of God's image begins within him, the born-again believer is part of the church which, in Bullinger's opinion, is a continuation of the early church by the acceptance of the Chalcedonian Creed,[35] Christ's twofold nature, and the actual achievement of salvation through the complete ransom of the human being. Christ is the foundation of the church, Bullinger writes, and it is in the church that the believer demonstrates his salvation by partaking in the Lord's Supper alongside the other believers who make up the body of Christ as a sign of love for one another and for Christ. Hence Daniël Timmerman emphasized that, according to Bullinger, "the Eucharist should not be used to coerce, deter, or excommunicate people," but "a joyful celebration."[36] Through this participation, the believer remembers Christ's suffering and death thus confirming that the Lord's Supper is a symbolic commemoration of Christ's sacrifice through which the whole church confesses its faith in God.

ASSESSMENT QUESTIONS

1. What does Zwingli say about Christ and the church?
2. How does Zwingli explain God's sovereignty?

---

33. Fesko, *Beyond Calvin*, 181.
34. Hildebrand, "Heinrich Bullinger (1504–1575) and the Covenant of Works," 259.
35. Drake, *Flesh of the Word*, 122.
36. Timmerman, *Heinrich Bullinger on Prophecy*, 202.

3. What does Zwingli refer to when he says that very Christian must be a God-taught person?
4. How does Bullinger describe God's election for salvation?
5. What is Bullinger's opinion regarding justification?

7

Reformed Theology (2)
Jean Calvin and Pietro Martire Vermigli

OBJECTIVES

1. To get acquainted with Calvin's doctrine of Scripture;
2. To know the main aspects of Calvin's doctrine of God;
3. To become accustomed to Calvin's doctrine of faith;
4. To identify the essential components of Pietro Martire's doctrine of justification;
5. To recognize Pietro Martire's doctrine of predestination and his sacramental theology.

Key words: Calvin, Vermigili, Scripture, faith, justification, predestination

JEAN CALVIN (1509–1564)

A second-generation reformer and undoubtedly "the most prominent and influential religious leader in the French orbit," as Raymond Mentzer describes him,[1] Calvin was influenced by a series of Reformed and Lutheran colleagues with whom he constantly kept in touch during his life, such as Martin Bucer, Guillaume Farel, Heinrich Bullinger, and Philip Melanchthon, to namely only the most famous theologians who left a decisive

---

1. Mentzer, "Calvin and France," 78.

imprint on Calvin's thought especially in the field of systematic theology. Barbara Pitkin demonstrates that in his most popular book, *Institutio religionis christianae* (The Teaching of the Christian Religion), Calvin followed closely Melanchthon's methodology used in his *Loci communes* (Fundamental Principles).[1]

The most important aspect of Calvin's theology is probably the importance he ascribes to the doctrine of Scripture which, Randall Zachman tells us, Calvin read "in the context of his understanding of the nature and activity of God."[2] Thus, he frequently underlines that we must read Scripture in order to know God and implicitly to worship in correctly. Scripture must be read personally by every Christian under the permanent guidance of pious and godly people, namely the pastors or presbyters. Calvin insists that Scripture must be read not only to know the correct doctrine, but also to always live according to God's commands revealed in Scripture. Likewise, Calvin says, Scripture must be read by the whole church. Carolyn Nystrom even claims that Calvin advocated that Scripture should be read aloud during the church's gathering.[3]

It is crucial to notice that all believers must read Scripture because every Christian exists in the church like a student in school, an image David Steinmetz discusses in one of his works.[4] The church is the school where we all learn about God and the textbook from which we learn everything we need to know about him is the Holy Scripture; this manual is permanently used by pastors and presbyters who are, according to Calvin, our teachers. Scripture must never be discontinued in the Christian's daily training for spiritual life and work because nobody knows how to work for God unless he finds out directly from Scripture under the spiritual and pedagogical guidance of pastors and presbyters in their role as spiritual rulers.[5]

Then, the next essential feature of Calvin's theology is the doctrine of God, which T. H. L. Parker discusses at length in his classical book about the subject.[6] Calvin presents God from the very beginning in his capacity as creator. Thus, as Charles Partee also points out, God is first and foremost

---

1. Pitkin, "Redefining Repentance: Calvin and Melanchthon," 276.
2. Zachman, *John Calvin as Teacher, Pastor, and Theologian*, 107.
3. Nystrom, *John Calvin*, 6.
4. Steinmetz, *Calvin in Context*.
5. Wait, *Great Challenges of Reformation Europe*, 125.
6. Parker, *Calvin's Doctrine of the Knowledge of God*.

the creator of heaven and earth, as well as the creator of the entire universe.[7] Last but not least, God is the creator of the human being, of each one of us; moreover, God himself got involved personally in our creation. In studying Scripture, Calvin notices that the human being was created as God's image; in fact, God's image, he believes, is visible in every human being even if the rest of creation bears and, as Nico Vorster puts it, "reflects God's image"[8] to a certain degree as well.

The reflection of God's image in creation, namely in the human being and the universe, urges us all, as Christians, to acquire the true knowledge of God through the reading of Scripture and meditation about the truths of Scripture. These spiritual exercises should raise our minds and hearts to God who keeps both in spiritual soundness and physical sanity. It is then quite easy to understand why Alister McGrath depicts Calvin as a promotor of a genuine natural theology[9] which affirms that every Christian should marvel at the greatness of the universe through contemplation because this urges us to (1) put our trust in God, (2) ask God for everything we need, (3) thank God for everything he gives us, and (4) obey God with all our hearts.

Because of sin, however, God cannot be fully known exclusively through the contemplation of the universe, namely through the mediation provided by divine revelation in nature, no matter how skillful God is presented by his harmonious, beautiful, and ordered creation.[10] Moreover, because of sin, we are no longer capably of correctly assessing God's revelation in nature. Consequently, we understand from Paul Helm's arguments that, in Calvin, if we truly want to know God, we need not only the glasses of Scripture but also the inner illumination provided by the Holy Spirit's internal testimony[11] which works within us.

Thus, according to Calvin, Scripture informs us on (1) God's spiritual and infinite essence or nature, (2) God's Trinitarian character as Father, Son, and Holy Spirit who share the same divine substance, (3) the generosity of God who gave us everything even before he created us, and (4) the constant care of God who never ceases to love us and keep us despite our sins. Greg Kame shows that these sins originate in Adam's voluntary

---

7. Partee, *Theology of John Calvin*, 51–52.
8. Vorster, *Brightest Mirror of God's Works*.
9. McGrath, *Christian Theology*.
10. Milner, *Calvin's Doctrine of the Church*, 10.
11. Helm, *John Calvin's Ideas*, 279.

transgression[12] which affected not only our capacity to see God in nature but also the very core of nature's physical constitution.

Nevertheless, Calvin points out, God can be known but the true knowledge of God presupposes at least two aspects: (1) God is good and full of love as creator of all things and (2) God is full of wrath against sin which he must punish by necessity. We find all these things in the gospel; in fact, the preaching of the gospel focuses our attention to the true image of God. In Calvin, as we read in John Leith, the true image of God is Jesus Christ,[13] who took our sins upon himself in accepting the curse, death, and eternal condemnation on our behalf by allowing himself to be crucified and suffer death in our place. According to Calving, Christ's work is the foundation of justification which consists of Christ's righteousness:

> A man is said to be justified in the sight of God when in the judgment of God, he is deemed righteous, and is accepted on account of his righteousness; for as iniquity is abominable to God, so neither can the sinner find grace in his sight, so far as h is and so long as he is regarded as a sinner . . . A man will be justified by faith when, excluded from the righteousness of works, he by faith lays hold of the righteousness of Christ, and clothed in it appears in the sight of God not as a sinner, but as righteous. Thus, we simply interpret justification, as the acceptance with which God receives us into his favor as if we were righteous; and we say that this justification consists in the forgiveness of sins and the imputation of the righteousness of Christ.[14]

In Calvin's theology the cross of Christ—a doctrine Ronald Wallace presents as "central" to Calvin's thought[15]—reveals that God himself placed sin and the guilt of sin upon Christ, so the entire work of salvation is nothing but God's initiative and his direct action in and through Christ. Thus, Christ's resurrection and ascension to heaven shows us clearly that God put everything we lack in Christ so that we should search only for him. Every Christian has the duty to look for God in and through Christ if the truly wants to be saved from his sins and if he genuinely wants to know God as he is in reality.

---

12. Kame, *Predestination*.
13. Leith, *John Calvin's Doctrine of the Christian Life*, 72.
14. Calvin, *Institutes of the Christian Religion*, 475.
15. Wallace, *Calvin's Doctrine of The Christian Life*, 43.

On the other hand, in Calvin's theology, the knowledge of God and salvation cannot be obtained without faith; in fact, they can be acquired exclusively by faith, which is also the only way to understand God according to his revelation in Scripture. Pieter Rouwendal highlight's Calvin presentation of faith as "a firm and certain knowledge of God's benevolence towards us,"[16] so faith as an epistemic role in Calvin's soteriological system. Faith is also necessary to benefit from the results of Christ's work on the cross, namely the forgiveness of sins and eternal life. Faith, Calvin insists, works out our union with Christ based on God's grace through repentance and justification. As a matter of fact, these two aspects constitute the very essence of grace, *duplex gratia Christi*,[17] and they are given to us by faith which unfortunately is never strong enough because of sin.

In order to strengthen us in faith, God decided to establish the church and it is within the church that every believer enjoys spiritual blessings alongside his brothers and sisters in the faith. However, Yosep Kim reminds us that these spiritual blessings must be enjoyed "in an eschatological way."[18] The church teaches us all about the reality of Christ's death and resurrection, as well as the reality of living with him through baptism and the Lord's Supper. In Calvin's theology, as we see in Todd Billings, baptism is the image not only of Christ's death and resurrection,[19] but also of our adoption and acceptance in God's family, while the Lord's Supper is the image of our union with Christ by faith.

PIETRO MARTIRE VERMIGLI (1499–1562)

An Italian reformer born in Florence, Pietro Martire studied Protestant theology under the supervision of Juan de Valdes,[20] a Spanish Catholic who was very interested in the reformation of the Catholic church. As a result of such investigations, Pietro Martire eventually accepted the doctrine of justification by faith alone in 1540, most likely, as Mario Biagioni suggests, under the influence of Bernardino Ochino.[21] Also known as the mentor of the famous reformed theologian Girolamo Zanchi whom he guided to

16. Rouwendal, *Predestination and Preaching in Genevan Theology*, 56.
17. Istafanous, *Calvin's Doctrine of Biblical Authority*, xxxvi.
18. Kim, *Identity and the Life of the Church*.
19. Billings, *Calvin, Participation, and the Gift*, 75.
20. Jones, *Spiritual Reformers in the 16th and 17th Centuries*, 236.
21. Biagioni, *Radical Reformation and the Making of Modern Europe*, 34.

the writings of Bucer, Melancthon, Bullinger, and Calvin, Pietro Martire taught theology in Strasbourg, Oxford, and Zürich. Thus, Pietro Martire's influence was of paramount importance for the development of English Protestantism because one of his students, who also accompanied him to Zürich, was John Jewell, the spiritual patron of none other than Richard Hooker, who organized systematically the liturgical and dogmatic theology of the Church of England during the long reign of Elizabeth I.

According to Frank James, Pietro Martire attended the Colloquy of Poissy where he had informative discussions with many Catholic theologians one of which, Antonio Caracciolo, bishop of Troyes in Frances, was so impressed with his arguments that he joined the Reformed party to become the first Reformed bishop in the history of the French Reformed church.[22] All these happened because of Pietro Martire's interest in and careful exposition of the crucial doctrine of justification by faith alone, the foundation and central aspect not only of Reformed theology but also of the whole Protestant theology in general as we see in Chris Castaldo's study.[23]

Castaldo also indicates that although important, dogmatic issues were never Pietro Martire's main preoccupation in the study of the doctrine of justification which he decided to approach from a pastoral perspective.[24] As far as he was concerned, there are three fundamental presuppositions in the study of justification as doctrine: (1) good works do not save, (2) faith justifies, and (3) only faith justifies. Thus, justification is a legal or juridical decision issued by God himself; in other words, justification is a forensic decision taken by God within the reality of the Holy Trinity. Pietro Martire explains that justification is aimed at the cancellation of the guilt of sin through a divine decision based on which God considers us righteous and innocent of our sins even if we are obviously not only sinful but also guilty of our sins. In other words, as John Patrick Donnelly proves, Martire's justification is explained in conjunction with his hamartiology.[25]

Nevertheless, in order to be able to consider us innocent of our sins, God imputes Christ's righteousness to us, namely he considers Christ's innocence to be ours even if it is not in reality. Thus, Heber Carlos de Campos provides a detailed analysis of Martire's doctrine of justification consisting of the non-imputation of sins, which means that God decides not to take

22. James, "Introduction," xxii.
23. Castaldo, *Justified in Christ*, 62.
24. Castaldo, *Justified in Christ*, 22.
25. Donnelly, *Calvinism and Scholasticism in Vermigli's Doctrine of Man and Grace*.

our sins into account before counting us sinless.[26] Justification, therefore, is a double reality as it resides in the (1) non-imputation of our sins and the (2) imputation of Christ's righteousness. The consequence of justification is double as well because we obtain the (1) forgiveness of sins and (2) eternal life, which we both receive from God by faith alone.

Pietro Martire explains justification by means of the concept of adoption, as we also read in John Fesko's analysis of his thought,[27] so it is through justification that we are accepted in God's family. Justification is not exclusively a forensic reality; it is also relational because all those who are justified enter a brand-new relationship with God and in doing, which means they all become his children. As far as Pietro Martire is concerned, an issue Jason Zuidema also confirms,[28] Christ's righteousness is external to the human being as it comes from outside (*extra nos*). Even though it is imputed to us as if it were ours, it remains forever external to us. Christ's righteousness remains Christ's despite that God considers it ours as if it were indeed ours. Here is how Pietro Martire views justification as adoption:

> We now have the Holy Scriptures which teach that the Heavenly Father reconciled himself with the human beings by no other means than the sacrifice of his only-begotten Son, by which he made an eternal pact with himself in order to forgive their sins, to adopt them as God's children, to given them unto salvation and care to his only-begotten Son so that they are incorporated into him, and finally to make them heirs of the kingdom of heaven ... the mystery of our redemption, performed by means of God's incarnate word ... and by the sacrifice of Christ offered on the altar of the cross ... for the remission of sins.[29]

In discussing the doctrine of justification, Pietro Martire also writes about the new birth and sanctification, a connection also indicated by Frank James.[30] The new birth and sanctification are both worked by God through the Holy Spirit who transforms Christ's righteousness imputed to us (but is not ours) into effective righteousness (which is ours). According to Richard Muller, in Pietro Martire, justification brings to our attention the doctrine

---

26. De Campos, *Doctrine in Development*.

27. Fesko, *Beyond Calvin*, 198.

28. Zuidema, *Peter Martyr Vermigli (1499–1562)*, 160.

29. Vermigli, *Discorso Di M. Pietro Martire Vermiglii Fiorentino*, 44–45.

30. James, "Theologies of Salvation in the Reformation and Counter-Reformation," 186.

of predestination,[31] which can be said to be identical to election. The cause of election is God's eternal will which, although the entire human race is sinful (*massa perditionis* in Augustin's theology) and cannot do anything for their salvation, is activated to decide the election of some individuals for salvation.

Consequently, Steven Murray argues that in Martire's thought, election is God's unconditional decision[32] based exclusively on his mercy and love, namely on his grace and benevolence, as Pietro Martire is very careful to explain without hesitation. As far as he is concerned, salvation consists of five distinct stages: (1) the election of some people from the totality of sinners, (2) the illumination worked by the Holy Spirit, (3) the reception of faith, (4) the acceptance of Christ, and (5) the inheritance of eternal life. Pietro Martire also believes in the reality of election for eternal damnation which he describes though as the passive expression of God's sovereign will because he decides to actively elect some people since he knows precisely what will happen unless he intervenes in human history. In this respect, Alexander Rosenthal supports the idea that Pietro Martire continues the medieval Catholic tradition which promotes the doctrine of double predestination as evident in the writings of Gregory of Rimini.[33]

Another vital issue for Pietro Martire's thought is sacramental theology, which Salvatore Corda presents as "closely interwoven with a rich variety of other theological motifs, such as the doctrine of revelation, Christology, and ecclesiology."[34] It is important to keep in mind that sacramental theology was a constant preoccupation for Pietro Martire since as early as his activity in Italy when, despite being a Catholic, he rejected three fundamental Catholic doctrines: (1) transubstantiation, (2) Christ's real and physical presence in bread and wine, and (3) the repeated sacrificing of Christ during the Eucharistic mass. In Pietro Martire's theology, as Stuart Clark tells us, the sacrament is the visible sign of an invisible grace,[35] which means that there is a clear distinction between (1) the sign (bread, wine) and (2) the reality designated by the sign (Christ's body and blood).

Thus, the bread and wine are the signs of Christ's presence while the sacraments speak of the believer's union with Christ. Yaroslav Viazovski

31. Muller, *Calvin and the Reformed Tradition*.
32. Murray, *Reclaiming Divine Wrath*, 145.
33. Rosenthal, *Crown under Law*, 29.
34. Corda, *Veritas Sacramenti*, 13.
35. Clark, *Vanities of the Eye*, 190.

claims that in Pietro Martire's thought, the doctrine of the union with Christ[36] has three distinct aspects which all underline the vital importance of Christ for the believer: (1) Christ's incarnation and his identification with humanity, (2) union with Christ which leads to sanctification, and (3) the mystical union with Christ whereby the believer partakes in the life of Christ, including through the Lord's Supper.

ASSESSMENT QUESTIONS

1. How does Calvin describe the importance of Scripture?
2. Which are the main elements of the doctrine of God in Calvin's theology?
3. How does Calvin present the role of faith?
4. What does justification consist of in Pietro Martire's theology?
5. Is there any connection between predestination and sacramental theology in Pietro Martire's thought?

---

36. Viazovski, *Image and Hope*, 84.

8

Reformed Theology (3)

Théodore de Bèze, Katharina Schütz Zell, and Martin Bucer

OBJECTIVES

1. To know the most important elements of Théodore de Bèze's doctrine of predestination;
2. To become familiarized with the role of women in Katharina Schütz Zell's theology;
3. To identify the importance of preaching in Katharina Schütz Zell's theology;
4. To appreciate Martin Bucer's doctrine of Christ's reign;
5. To learn about Martin Bucer's doctrine of Christ's threefold office.

Key words: de Bèze, Zell, Bucer, predestination, marriage, mediatory office (Christ as mediator), reign (Christ as Lord)

THÉODORE DE BÈZE (1519-1605)

A third-generation reformer, according to Pieter Rouwendal, de Bèze was Calvin's apprentice and successor at the leadership of the Genevan church as well as one of the most important Reformed theologians from the second half of the sixteenth century.[1] Considered the initiator of the so-called Reformed Orthodoxy, also known as Protestant Scholasticism, de Bèze continues classical Reformed theology based on an obviously rationalistic approach unlike his predecessors. The central theme of his theology is the doctrine of predestination, which is anchored in the conviction that God's providence, manifested in predestination, is the source of every believer's security and trust. It is important to understand, John Bray tells us, that de Bèze's doctrine of predestination is treated in a way which resembles philosophical methodologies[2] and, as we see in Suk Yu Chan, medieval scholastic theology.[3]

In this case, predestination must necessarily be the foundation of moral behavior in all Christians because the good works which must be performed by every believer originate in God's predestination and providence—and this is, according to Kirk Summers, a pastoral approach to both doctrines.[4] According to de Bèze, these teachings are clear in the Holy Scriptures, including the *Song of Songs* which in his theology becomes a sort of allegory of Christ's love for the church. Thus, Timothy Robinson suggests that, in de Bèze, the *Song of Songs* teaches us not to focus on our own person, but only on Jesus Christ, our Savior.[5]

Even if he insists on the doctrine of predestination, de Bèze is aware of the necessity of faith and repentance—in this order, is Graham Redding's warning[6]—for the salvation of each believer. This is because the plan God initiated from eternity is far too complex for human understanding and reason, while the divine commands which deal with faith and repentance must be followed within the general context of predestination. As far as de Bèze is concerned, as we see in Baird Tipson, the doctrine of predestination consists of two parts: (1) God's eternal decision to do a certain thing and (2) the application of God's eternal decision within the history of humankind in a concrete way.[7]

De Bèze explains that justification is part of the application of God's eternal decision in history; this is why every Christian must be fully aware

---

1. Rouwendal, *Predestination and Preaching in Genevan Theology*, 86.
2. Bray, *Theodore Beza's Doctrine of Predestination*, 161.
3. Chan, *Heavenly Providence*, 171.
4. Summers, *Morality After Calvin*, 352.
5. Robinson, "Banquet of Love," 352.
6. Redding, *Prayer and the Priesthood of Christ*, 145.
7. Tipson, *Inward Baptism*, 177ff.

of this extremely important reality for his own life and salvation seen—we read in McGrath—as absolution of sins through Christ's death.[8] Predestination is not based on God's foreknowledge of our works because this would ultimately mean that salvation is by work and if Scripture affirms the primacy of grace, not of works, for salvation, then any explanation must take this aspect into account. Thus, predestination must be considered from a totally different angle which excludes works as source of salvation. However, as de Bèze himself writes, justification profoundly alters man's psyche and his actions:

> in the Gospel only, Christ that our only mediator is declared unto us to be made righteousness of God the Father . . . the spirit of regeneration is always annexed with the gift of righteousness by imputation, which is received by faith, which does kindle in the hearts of them that are justified an earnest loathing of sin, hope, true obedience, and other virtues. Whereof this follows, that the conscience being pacified, doth enjoy a true and perpetual joy, what storms sour do arise.[9]

It is now clear why de Bèze is convinced that predestination is based on God's grace and benevolence which are manifested as mercy towards all those whom God wants to elect for salvation.[10] Regarding predestination, de Bèze writes that it has two main causes: (1) a primary cause, namely God's goodness and grace, and (2) a secondary cause, or faith and the gospel call. Scripture has a decisive role in predestination because it focuses our attention to at least three vital aspects: (1) the necessity of faith, (2) the person and work of Christ, and (3) the purpose and the eternal plan of God—which was set in motion, Brian Moynahan argues, "before Adam" with its corresponding "election and damnation."[11]

In de Bèze, predestination manifests itself through election and election becomes effective through faith. Nevertheless, Jeffrey Mallinson shows that both are possible due to Christ's death on the cross whose purpose is our reconciliation with God,[12] a reality worked exclusively by God. Thus, de Bèze explains that the election, the calling, the justification, and the sanctification of believers are accomplished by God alone, not by us.

---

8. McGrath, *Iustitia Dei*, 226.
9. de Bèze, *Psalmes of David*, 54.
10. Rouwendal, *Predestination and Preaching in Genevan Theology*, 182.
11. Moynahan, *Faith*, 393.
12. Mallinson, *Faith, Reason, and Revelation in Theodore Beza*, 222.

A Very Brief Introduction to Reformation Doctrine

Despite the rationalism used to explain the connection between predestination and justification, as well as between God's eternal plan and its application in history, de Bèze makes frequent references to Scripture. This is his attempt to prove that God commands us to read his Word not only for the understanding of faith and repentance, but also—as we can read in Raymond Blacketer—for "Christian living."[13]

KATHARINA SCHÜTZ ZELL (1498-1562)

Raised and brought up in a Catholic spirit in the city of Strasbourg, Katharina became a nun at the tender age of ten. According to Marjorie Plummer, in 1521, when Martin Luther was excommunicated from the Catholic church of Rome, Mathias Zell arrives Strasbourg and he begins to preach in a Lutheran or Evangelical style. Katharina understands the message of the gospel and, according to her own confession, finds peace for her soul. Four years later, in 1525, she marries Mathias Zell in order to apply, as practically as possible, the new teachings about the understanding of Scripture which evidently aimed at clerical marriage or, to be more precise, the possibility of marital life for the priests and the monks of the Catholic church of Rome.[14]

Katharina and Mathias were always ready to see and follow the things which unite Christians, not those who produce schism and division, for as long as the Christian faith was not damaged and the gospel was not distorted by false teachings. Consequently, we read in Elsie McKee that both considered themselves colleagues of Luther, Zwingli, Schwenckfeld, but also of the "poor Baptist brethren"[15]—in fact, the Anabaptists—who were severely persecuted by everybody: Catholics, Lutherans, and the Reformed. Furthermore, although Protestants, their house was always open and available not only to all sorts of Evangelicals but also to Catholics, with whom they engaged in vivid conversations even if they never hesitated to criticize their theology, which they saw as dogmatically deficient.

Because she was a woman, Katharina was not allowed to actually preach the gospel, but she did write on a rather large range of subjects, such as (1) clerical marriage, (2) the priesthood of all believers, and (3) the role of women, children, and lay people for the education of families and communities unto the Christian faith. Following Mathias's death in

13. Blacketer, "Man in the Black Hat," 239.
14. Plummer, *From Priest's Whore to Pastor's Wife*, 228.
15. McKee, *Katharina Schütz Zell*, 1:106–7.

Reformed Theology (3)

1548, Katharina not only wrote about the manifestation of God's mercy in the midst of troubles and sufferings but also, as John Derksen points out, "threw herself even more into caring for the suffering."[16] Towards the end of her life, Katharina was interested in the relationship between Christ as savior (salvation by grace alone) and the preaching of God's gospel by the church through word and deed. After all, as Katharina said in her own words, our entire Christian life depends on Christ and his work:

> Our second Adam (Christ) was obedient to you (Father) and reconciled us to you on the wood (cross). He humbled himself and died as a man. He also bore penance for us and suffered in the body that you had prepared for him. Through that he freed us from the prison of the hellish bond of sins and justified us in his resurrection and brought us to living resurrection and overcame eternal death. He also opened the closed-up heaven of your favor and grace and set himself as the first at your right hand to prepare a place for us. And he will come again to gather us there, yes, all those who give themselves to him and remain in him, and to punish and show his power in those who have torn themselves from him and have not remained in his life.[17]

Katharina was convinced that the only authority for ecclesiastical doctrine and practice is the Holy Scripture as fully inspired by God. The opinions of theologians do not matter, and they are most certainly not inspired but everybody, both clerics and laity, must apply the gospel by preaching Christ as the only savior of humankind. As far as Katharina is concerned, salvation cannot be obtained by doing good works or by receiving the sacraments, because sin consists of unbelief, namely one's lack of trust in Christ. Consequently, McKee confirms that, in Katharina's mind, salvation can only be obtained by faith alone and faith means trust in Christ,[18] as we find out in Scripture, the only theological authority for all Christians.

Pneumatology is important for Katharina because the Holy Spirit does talk to people, but he does it exclusively through Scripture. Merry Wiesner reveals that, according to Katharina, there was a "standard" for the pneumatic Christian living, namely that a believer should be filled with the Holy Spirit.[19] Every Christian has the duty to read and study Scripture

---

16. Derksen, *From Radicals to Survivors*, 239.
17. Schütz Zell, *Church Mother*, 158.
18. McKee, *Katharina Schütz Zell*, 75.
19. Wiesner, *Women and Gender in Early Modern Europe*, 240.

for his or her own life. Likewise, every Christian must preach, or tell others about the biblical faith we all find in Scripture. Katharina believed that faith should be learned, and this learning process must be not only an individual exercise but also a communitarian endeavor. Thus, the church must manifest its faith through baptism,[20] including infant baptism, even if the latter must never be seen as washing sins, but only as the infant's entrance into the covenant of grace.

Also, the church must manifest its faith through the Lord's Supper, a wonderful occasion for brotherly communion and fellowship when Christians remember Christ's sacrifice by listening to the preaching of God's word. In every church the preacher must proclaim the gospel based on Scripture, not argue against or quarrel with other preaches regarding issues of secondary or no importance. What truly matters for Katharina, who thus demonstrates her credentials as a Reformed theologian, is the actual preaching of the Scripture's doctrines, even if this means that preachers and pastors are to be elected by the city council, namely the authorities of the state, and even if the government oversees the activity of the church by law. Moreover, Päivi Räisänen-Schröder reminds us that, according to Katharina, preaching had a pedagogical component because "bad teachings were doing more harm than bad living, as teachings had a broader effect on people than individual conduct."[21]

Katharina also writes about faith, which he describes as constantly manifesting by necessity, in everyday life, as practically as possible. Moreover, faith must always be accompanied by love.[22] The Christian has the duty to love everybody; in fact, he must love everybody. This is why Katharina never approved of the persecution and execution of Anabaptists or of the highly inflammatory quarrels, theological or not, between various Protestant theologians. Consequently, she believed that Scripture cannot be understood correctly unless it is constantly read in faith and humility. Katharina was convinced that women have a decisive and beneficial role in the church even if, as Nathan Mitchell explains, she disapproved of women ordination to ecclesiastical ministry.[23]

---

20. McKee, *Katharina Schütz Zell*, 245.

21. Räisänen-Schröder, "Appeal and Survival of Anabaptism in Early Modern Germany," 124.

22. McKee, *Katharina Schütz Zell*, 365.

23. Mitchell, "Reforms, Protestant and Catholic," 331.

Regardless of whether one is ordained or not, every Christian must defend the truth of the gospel if this is misrepresented. Thus, all Christians have the foremost duty to defend the truth of the gospel in order to (1) honor God's teachings as revealed in Scripture and to (2) make sure he or she has a clear conscience by not promoting lies. This is why all Christians must preach the gospel through word and deed; the preaching of the gospel, however, must always be simple if it is to be understood by everybody.[24]

Katharina was convinced that the preaching of the gospel is vital because it offers access to (1) the knowledge of the Word (Scripture and Christ) and to (2) faith in Christ. John Thompson writes that Katharina herself possessed "a formidable knowledge of Scripture, and her writings are filled with quotations, paraphrases, and allusions to most of the books of the Bible."[25] If they truly want to know how to preach the gospel, Christians must look at Christ himself who not only provided an example for everybody to follow in this respect but also was ready to suffer so that all people have the chance to hear God's true word. If Christ himself was willing to suffer, and he did suffer for all of us, then we must also be ready to suffer for the sake of others. And the first step in that direction, as Ronald Rittgers writes about Katharina, is to console those who find themselves amid suffering.[26]

MARTIN BUCER (1491-1551)

Famous for his contribution to the reformation of the church in the city of Strasbourg and, in the last two years of his life, for this teaching activity at the University of Cambridge, as we find out from Wilhelm Pauck, Martin Bucer is one of the most esteemed reformers of the sixteenth century.[27] Even if he sided with Luther since as early as 1518, Bucer eventually decided to join Zwingli's reformation in 1524 when he became officially a Reformed theologian. Preoccupied mainly with Christology, Willem van 't Spiker shows that Bucer was interested in Christ's office as mediator,[28] which not only constitutes the foundation of the doctrine of believers' priesthood but also explains the reality of justification. In Bucer's words:

24. McKee, *Katharina Schütz Zell*, 91.
25. Thompson, "Rules Proved by Exceptions," 534.
26. Rittgers, *Reformation of Suffering*, 237.
27. Pauck, *Melanchthon and Bucer*, 159.
28. van 't Spijker, *Ecclesiastical Offices in the Thought of Martin Bucer*, 61.

> We require that the chief doctrine of Christianity be taught clearly and continually, that the remission of sins and eternal salvation is based on the sole mercy of God and merit of Christ, and not upon any of our merit, and that we secure eternal life by faith not good works, although God generously rewards good works to us by the same boundless and gratuitous love and merit of his son with good things both in the present and the future, however these are the works of Christ within us.[29]

Especially interested in the work of Christ and not necessarily in his person because this was considered a done deal since Patristic times (when the Council of Chalcedon issued its famous christological symbol in 451), Bucer accepted without reservation Christ's twofold nature as God incarnate in a person with two distinct natures: divine and human.[30] Thus, he decided to focus on Christ's work because this was the sole means to achieve salvation from sin. Bucer was convinced that salvation depended first and foremost on the knowledge of Christ as a historical process framed by creation and the end thereof. Likewise, we read in Sujin Pak, he believed that the work of Christ restores all things to their original state, to the order which they were all created for, and that happens through "Christ's restoration of the elect."[31]

Bucer insists on the fact that salvation refers predominantly to our reconciliation with God, as Andrew Purves explains us;[32] this, however, cannot and should not be limited to Christ's propitiation by his death on the cross. On the contrary, reconciliation must also include the restoration of all things to the glory they had when they were created. According to van 't Spijker, this cosmic perspective on salvation causes Bucer to believe that Christ's mediatory work will come to an end when the elect willfully enjoy the future glory of salvation,[33] which will thoroughly transform the entire creation because of Christ's reign over it.

Jonathon Beeke mentions that the idea of Christ's reign (*regnum Christi*) is crucial for Bucer's theology[34] and presupposes not only (1) Christ's office as king (Christ as king), but also (2) Christ's ascension to heaven following his humiliation through his execution and death on the cross.

---

29. Lugioyo, *Martin Bucer's Doctrine of Justification*, 153.
30. Derksen, *From Radicals to Survivors*, 80.
31. Pak, *Judaizing Calvin*, 64.
32. Purves, *Pastoral Theology in the Classical Tradition*, 88.
33. van 't Spijker, *Ecclesiastical Offices in the Thought of Martin Bucer*, 40.
34. Beeke, *Duplex Regnum Christi*, 75.

Bucer believes that Christ rules the entire world in his capacity as creator *logos*, as David Hopper specifies,[35] so Christ can also be known through the mediation of creation, although true knowledge Christ can only be achieved by the contemplation of the cross which we find in Scripture. As a priest, prophet, and king,[36] Christ has a threefold office (*munus triplex*) through which the rules the entire world based on the assistance provided by the Holy Spirit.

Christ, therefore, is sovereign over the entire creation in Bucer's theology—we find from Scott Dixon,[37] even if his sovereignty is mainly intrinsic or internal to the human being due to the work of the Holy Spirit in believers, namely in the church. As far as Bucer is concerned, the church is Christ's spiritual kingdom and has the following signs: (1) the correct preaching of the gospel, (2) the correct administration of sacraments, (3) public worship, and (4) discipline (forgiveness of sins in the name of Christ as well as the excommunication of sinner and their re-acceptance based on repentance and forgiveness). Because of Christ's sovereignty over the whole world, Bucer is in favor of the cooperation between church and state or, in the words of J. T. McNeill, he did not assert the autonomy of the church as over against the state."[38] This is why he explains that the church must be governed by (1) the pastor, (2) presbyters, and (3) the church clerk (*Kirchenpfleger*) as representative of the state (in fact, in Bucer's time, he represented only the city council).

ASSESSMENT QUESTIONS

1. What does de Bèze say about predestination?
2. What where Katharina Schütz Zell's main theological interests?
3. What is the role of women in the church according to Katharina Schütz Zell's theology?
4. How does Bucer describe Christ's office as mediator?
5. How does Bucer present Christ's reign and the cooperation between church and state?

---

35. Hopper, *Divine Transcendence and the Culture of Change*, 132.
36. van 't Spijker, *Ecclesiastical Offices in the Thought of Martin Bucer*, 40.
37. Dixon, *Protestants*, 64.
38. McNeill, *History and Character of Calvinism*, 163.

9

Reformed Theology (4)
Thomas Cranmer and Richard Hooker

OBJECTIVES

1. To understand the main characteristics of Cranmer's theology;

2. To identify the relationship between justification, faith, and good works in Cranmer's theology;

3. To comprehend the connection between predestination and election in Cranmer's theology;

4. To apprehend Hooker's doctrines of faith, sin, and grace;

5. To recognize the importance of Hooker's concept of ecclesiastical law.

Key words: Cranmer, Hooker, laws, liturgy, righteousness, faith

THOMAS CRANMER (1489–1556)

Cranmer is one of the most important and world-famous English reformers. Educated at the University of Cambridge, Cranmer came across the first reformation ideas within a humanist group of scholars dominated by Erasmus's overwhelming influence. Erasmus's philology encouraged Cranmer to study biblical theology or, as Roger Olson says, to open "the Bible to the people,"[1] so Cranmer found himself in the position of knowing and

---

1. Olson, *Story of Christian Theology*, 436.

defending the doctrine of justification by faith alone relatively early in his theological career. Famous for his *Book of the Common Prayer*,[2] Cranmer produced this liturgical work of paramount importance for the worship of the Church of England out of his determination to reform not only the doctrines but also the life of the church, and he found ecclesiastical worship to be an appropriate starting point in this direction.

One of his most important works is his *Notes on Justification*, in which Cranmer clarifies the issue of justification by pointing out that its foundation is not even faith but rather God's grace and benevolence, as we are told by Ashley Null, for our reconciliation with him.[3] The doctrine of justification must never underscore the believer's faith, but the fact that justification is possible only because of God who works through grace. Thus, Cranmer indicates that justification is essentially and exclusively God's work through Christ, and this must never be overshadowed by people's works or even good works which possess no soteriological value whatsoever. Here is a presentation of Cranmer's understanding of justification:

> in our justification by Christ it is not all one thing, the office of God unto man, and the office of man unto God. Justification is not the office of man, but of God: for man cannot justify himself by his own works, neither in part, nor in the whole; for that were the greatest arrogancy and presumption of man that antichrist could erect against God, to affirm that a man might by his own works take away and purge his own sins, and so justify himself. But justification is the office of God only, and is not a thing which we render unto him, but which we receive of him; not which we give him, but which we take of him, by his free mercy and by the only merits of his most dearly-beloved Son, our only Redeemer, Saviour, and Justifier, Jesus Christ.[4]

Cranmer makes it clear that human works do not qualify soteriologically in any way, and they can never have any value for salvation to such a degree that they might acquire merits for the forgiveness of sins. Only Christ's work based on his sacrifice on the cross is capable of obtaining sufficient merits for the forgiveness and cancellation of sins; so nobody but Christ himself is capable of doing anything at all for the salvation of men and women. Human beings, therefore, can do nothing in this respect as Susan

---

2. Jacobs, *Book of Common Prayer*.
3. Null, *Thomas Cranmer's Doctrine of Repentance*, 209.
4. Cranmer, *Works of Thomas Cranmer*, 131.

Wabuda emphasizes rather poignantly.[5] Justification by faith alone brings to light Christ's fundamental importance for salvation as initiated by God, not by people.

In Cranmer's thought, justification is achieved by God himself for the sake of Christ and the human being can only appropriate justification by faith for himself. This concrete reality of faith, which manifests itself within the human being, allows men and women to acknowledge Christ's merits for justification, not their own. By faith, the human being realizes not only that he has no merits for salvation, but also that he is utterly incapable of doing anything for it, so faith helps the human being to trust God alone, the only one who can give him salvation based on Christ's sacrifice. In this respect, Peter Toon confirms that, in Cranmer, "justification is wholly the gift of God."[6]

This is in fact the very definition of grace: God saves the human being despite the latter's sins. In his *Homilies*, Cranmer underlines the importance of God's benevolence for justification by proving that God makes the first step towards human salvation. God's soteriological initiative can be seen in justification, which is based on Christ's righteousness and innocence, not in the human being who lacks both; whatever the believer has is insufficient for his salvation.[7] Patrick Collinson draws our attention to Christ's righteousness,[8] which in Cranmer is the foundation of justification. Also, it remains forever external to the human being as unshakable foundation which (1) emphasizes God's grace and (2) cancels God's wrath.

According to Samuel Leuenberger, Cranmer describes justification by means of the concept of ransom,[9] which was paid by Christ to fulfill the requirements of God's justice. It is interesting to see that even if he allots considerable time to justification and Christ's righteousness, Cranmer does not mention the imputation of Christ's righteousness; he does use the concept, however, for the believer's righteousness. Thus, in Cranmer's theology, justification presupposed two essential aspects: (1) the forgiveness of sins and (2) the reconciliation of the believer with God or renewal in Christ. Ian Hussey correctly notices that, in Cranmer, these two aspects of

---

5. Wabuda, *Thomas Cranmer*.
6. Toon, *Justification and Sanctification*, 91–92.
7. Simuţ, *Doctrine of Salvation in the Sermons of Richard Hooker*, 88.
8. Collinson, *From Cranmer to Sancroft*, 21.
9. Leuenberger, *Archbishop Cranmer's Immortal Bequest*, 112.

justification constitute the rock of the Christian religion.[10] Justification is strongly pneumatological because the believer is able to do good works as a result of justification only because of the Holy Spirit's inner activity and his indwelling within the believer.

One of Cranmer's constant preoccupations was to underline that justification can be achieved by faith alone,[11] or exclusively by faith without any other help; he insisted on this to counter Catholic teachings. At the beginning of the sixteenth century, Catholic churches accepted that justification was by faith, but—as we learn from Timothy George—in Catholic theology faith was always associated with hope and love which, in turn, leads to good works.[12] Consequently, according to Cranmer, justification by faith in Catholic theology automatically refers to justification by works, while in Cranmer nothing outside faith is capable of contributing to justification.

Faith, however, is not a work of justification or a good work performed for justification because the human being cannot obtain justification on his own. In Cranmer, all the human being can do is receive, by faith alone, God's justification as a work God himself gives him by grace. Stephen Spencer reminds us that justification by grace was one of the things of which Cranmer was never "unsure."[13] This means that, as far as Cranmer is concerned, faith has epistemological value. By faith, the human being knows God and knowing God leads to good works which are the genuine proof of faith and justification. Although faith may appear as pertaining to human psychology, it is certainly God's gift. Thus, as God's gift,[14] faith is an external reality to the human being, but it manifests itself within men and women by means of their psyche.

In Cranmer's view, Null points out, faith is indeed God's gift but only for the elect.[15] Thus, from the perspective of election, faith produces in the believer the kind of security which allows him to be kept in grace until the end. Sinful human nature will push the believer towards evil actions, but God's faithfulness will always bring him back on the right track. This is why, in Cranmer, the perseverance of the saints in grace[16] is the cause

10. Hussey, *Soteriological Use of Call by Paul and Luke*, 39.
11. Hicks, *Worship by Faith Alone*.
12. George, *Galatians*.
13. Spencer, *SCM Studyguide to Anglicanism*, 19.
14. Locke, *Church in Anglican Theology*.
15. Null, *Thomas Cranmer's Doctrine of Repentance*, 129.
16. Null, *Thomas Cranmer's Doctrine of Repentance*, 224.

of good works which are the demonstration of the believer's gratitude for God's grace.

RICHARD HOOKER (1553–1600)

Hooker is undoubtedly the most important theologian of the Church of England in the sixteenth century and is rightfully considered the founder of Anglican theology. Until the twentieth century, scholars believed that Hooker was the promoter of the middle way (the so-called *via media*) between Geneva's Reformed theology and Rome's Catholic theology, an aspect which Aidan Nichols discusses in detail.[17] After 1950 and especially after 1990, Hooker's image within Anglican scholarship changed as some of the more recent works demonstrated his Reformed credentials in soteriology, like—for instance—in the works of Torrance Kirby,[18] even though he was never in agreement with Reformed Presbyterian ecclesiology which he dismissed in favor of Episcopalian church government.

Extremely interested in soteriology, Hooker criticizes the Catholic doctrine of salvation in his famous *Discourse on Justification* (1586) which belongs to the first stage of his career (1581–1593) when he published *Two Sermons on Jude, Sermon on the Security and Perpetuity of Faith in the Elect, Discourse on Justification*, and *Sermon on the Nature of Pride*. After 1593, in the second stage of his career, Hooker wrote the eight books of his renown *Laws of the Ecclesiastical Polity* as well as his celebrated *Dublin Fragments*.[19]

The first stage of his career has a specifically Reformed orientation,[20] while the second, and especially towards the end of his life, may appear to come closer to Catholic theology in the sense that his theology becomes poignantly sacramental, a feature of his theology which Charles Miller attributes to Hooker's use of the *Thirty-Nine Articles*.[21] It must be stressed here that even if the source of his theology was always Scripture, Hooker also acknowledged the importance of ecclesiastical tradition not only as part of church history but also as indicative of the perseverance of saints throughout history despite their individual or communitarian mistakes

---

17. Nichols, *The Panther and the Hind*, 47ff.
18. Kirby, *Richard Hooker, Reformer and Platonist*.
19. Simuț, *Richard Hooker and His Early Doctrine of Justification*.
20. Simuț, *Doctrine of Salvation in the Sermons of Richard Hooker*, 52.
21. Miller, *Richard Hooker and the Vision of God*.

Reformed Theology (4)

and regardless of the dogmatic or practical errors committed by the Catholic church of Rome and its believers.

Despite this concession made to Catholic theology and the Catholics in general, Hooker proposes a theology of justification which is based on the typically Protestant, Lutheran and Reformed, even Calvinistic, rejection of the idea that the human being can do some things to obtain his salvation. In this respect, Hooker is clear: the human being can do nothing for his salvation because of sin; nor can he do anything to merit it before God, Barbara Lewalski tells us.[22] On the contrary, he needs righteousness to benefit from justification which is exclusively God's work. Hooker, however, explains that righteousness is threefold: (1) the righteousness of justification, (2) the righteousness of sanctification, and (3) the righteousness of glorification—and they reflect God's decision to do something in order to provide satisfaction for our sins through faith in Christ:

> because God was thus to be satisfied, and man not able to make satisfaction, in such sort, his unspeakable love and inclination to save mankind from eternal death, ordained in our behalf a mediator to do that, which had been for any other impossible. Wherefore all sin is remitted in the only faith of Christ's passion, and no man, without belief thereof justified. Faith alone makes Christ's satisfaction ours: howbeit that faith alone which after sin, makes us by conversion his . . . we are in Christ made thereby capable, and fit vessels to receive the fruit of his satisfaction, yea we so far please and content God, that because when we have offended, he looks but for repentance at our hands: our repentance and the works thereof, are therefore termed satisfactory.[23]

In Hooker's theology, the key which opens the door to salvation is the righteousness of justification by faith alone for which the human being contributes nothing. Barry Smith confirms that, in Hooker, the righteousness of justification is not ours, but Christ's, so it is imputed.[24] Therefore, the human being cannot acquire any merits to obtain the necessary righteousness for justification. Only Christ has the necessary righteousness for the justification of sinners, but this is effective only for those found in him, namely the elect. In Hooker, the elect are included in Christ by *incorporatio*[25]

---

22. Lewalski, *Donne's Anniversaries and the Poetry of Praise*, 131.
23. Hooker, "Of the Laws of Ecclesiastical Polity, Book 1," 37.
24. Smith, *Meaning of Jesus' Death*, 96.
25. Hooker, *Works of Mr. Richard Hooker*, 263.

as soon as they appropriate the righteousness of justification by faith alone as God's gift, having already been elected to benefit from God's mercy and love.

According to Philip Secor, the righteousness of sanctification is the righteousness of those already justified, or considered righteous, and it helps them do good works as proof of their justification, which means the righteousness of sanctification is inherent.[26] Justified believers are accepted by God as righteous in Christ, not in themselves, so salvation is by grace while good works are the natural and necessary consequence of justification. In Hooker, faith is not the objective identification of the believer with Christ, but the subjective acknowledgment of the salvation performed by Christ and applied to the believer by grace. Thus, Miller acknowledges that, in Hooker, faith is God's gift,[27] which always points to Christ.

Predestination—which, according to Nigel Voak, does not contradict man's liberty in Hooker[28]—was one of Hooker's main interests towards the end of his life when he used to say that the correct understanding of sin was dependent on predestination. Paul Dominiak examines the issue of sin in conjunction with Hooker's distinction between free creation and sinful creation.[29] Before the fall, Hooker writes, God's initial plan for the human being was still his salvation (in fact, existence unto life eternal) based on his voluntary obedience to divine will. The human being, however, chose not to obey God, so sin entered the world through the voluntary choice of evil, not of divine will. In other words, sin entered the world with God's permission, not as a result of God's decision.

Hooker believes that the emergence of sin in the world awoke God's justice,[30] which would have otherwise remained asleep, as proof that the punishment of sin was never part of God's purpose for the human being. This is why it cannot be argued that God had predestined some for eternal damnation since sin entered the world through the human being's voluntary choice of evil. In Hooker's thought, as we see in David Neelands, predestination is connected to God's decision to punish sin, which means that sin the very cause of condemnation.[31]

26. Secor, *Richard Hooker*, 186.
27. Miller, *Richard Hooker and the Vision of God*.
28. Voak, *Richard Hooker and Reformed Theology*, 59.
29. Dominiak, *Richard Hooker*, 57.
30. Simuț, *Doctrine of Salvation in the Sermons of Richard Hooker*, 163.
31. Neelands, "Predestination," 202.

David Eppley holds that, in Hooker, predestination does not exclude the necessity of sanctification which is the duty of every believer.[32] Sanctification must be visible, at least liturgically, in his participation to the Lord's Supper. Hooker attempted to provide a coherent theology of the Lord's Supper which was meant to avoid the schismatic controversies already present among the Protestants. Paul Avis notices that, in Hooker, the Eucharist is meant to be a unifying factor because the sacrament "makes" the "mystical body of Christ."[33] Thus, Hooker indicates that, as a human being, Christ is not omnipresent (so one cannot defend the ubiquity of Christ's presence in the Lord's Supper, as in Lutheran theology); as God, however, his omnipresence is visible beyond any shred of doubt (so one can indeed argue in favor of Christ's presence at the Lord's Supper since his human nature coexists with his divine nature).

Decisively influenced by Elizabethan society and legislation, Hooker defines the church of Christ as the visible society of believers and a political body, an aspect Bradford Littlejohn investigates in connection with Hooker's justification and sanctification.[34] Like secular society, the church works based on laws and even if these laws are merely ecclesiastical, they do originate in God's will expressed in Scripture as a reality that directs "all things."[35] Hooker was convinced that there had to be a balance between secular and ecclesiastical laws because secular laws can support the dissemination of the church in the world. If secular society has certain laws which resemble ecclesiastical laws to some degree, then the church may be more easily accepted by society.

Nevertheless, it is vital for the ecclesiastical laws to be drafted based on Scripture because the Bible must always constitute the very foundation of ecclesiastical decisions. Kenneth Locke demonstrates that, in Hooker, Scripture must be read by the entire community of believers so that better decisions are taken, sometimes even to correct bishops.[36] Consequently, A. J. Joyce intimates that, in Hooker, the interpretation of Scripture must be based on the correct use of human reason aided by the work of the Holy Spirit.[37] In other words, as Hooker points out, human reason should always

---

32. Eppley, "Richard Hooker on the Un-Conditionality of Predestination," 72.
33. Avis, *Reconciling Theology*.
34. Littlejohn, *Richard Hooker*, 157.
35. Chibi, *Fear God, Honor the King*, 246.
36. Locke, *Church in Anglican Theology*.
37. Joyce, *Richard Hooker and Anglican Moral Theology*, 116.

be subject to divine reason, namely to the work of the Holy Spirit, which not only helps the human being to better use his reason, but also radically changes his way of thinking, a conviction which underscores Hooker's credentials as a Reformed theologian.

ASSESSMENT QUESTIONS

1. What is the definition of justification in Cranmer's theology?
2. What does Cranmer have to say about Christ's righteousness?
3. What is Cranmer's most famous liturgical achievement?
4. What does Hooker say about faith?
5. How does Hooker define the relationship between ecclesiastical laws and secular laws?

10

Catholic Theology (1)
Tomasso de Vio Cajetan and Thomas More

OBJECTIVES

1. To know Cajetan's career and his importance for the discussions with the Lutherans;
2. To know Cajetan's arguments in favor of a possible agreement with the Lutherans;
3. To know the most important doctrines in Cajetan's theology;
4. To know More's criticism against Evangelical theology;
5. To know the difference between biblical philology and theology in More's theology.

Key words: Cajetan, More, homiletics, sovereignty, tradition, Scripture

TOMASSO DE VIO CAJETAN (1469-1534)

Born in Gaeta (Caieta), close to Thomas Aquinas's birthplace, Cajetan is one of the most important Catholic theologians of the Reformation age. Baptized as Giacomo de Vio, as Michael Mullett tells us,[1] the future cardinal adopted the name Tomasso (Thomas) to honor Thomas Aquinas when he joined the ecclesiastical order of the Dominican monks. Franco Riva

---

1. Mullett, *Historical Dictionary of the Reformation and Counter-Reformation*, 50.

discloses a whole range of interesting aspects of Cajetan's activity,[2] but one of the most important is that he began his academic career at the University of Padova in 1491 where he taught Thomas Aquinas's theology and philosophy, according to the scientific curriculum of those times which was heavily influenced by late Medieval scholasticism.

Craig Martin explains that Cajatan was preoccupied by the doctrine of the immortality of the soul[3] within the context of the philosophical debates at the University of Padova. Specifically, he strove to provide philosophical arguments in favor of the idea that the soul can exists without the body after death. This philosophical but also eschatological interest force Cajetan to use the symmetry principle which postulates that between the angels' pure spirits and the realities that animate the lives of animals there must be a spiritual entity defined as the human spirit. We find out from John Finnis that Cajetan used the same methodology to discuss the symmetry of distributive and commutative justice.[4] Even if this conclusion is somewhat forced, Cajetan used it rather successfully in his university pursuits which aimed at combining scholastic theology and philosophy with the study of Scripture.

In 1497–1498, as Paul Grendler divulges, Cajetan leaves the University of Padova for the University of Pavia,[5] then the University of Milano where he continues to write commentaries on Aristotel's works. Francis Xavier Clooney explains that Cajetan also begins his commentary to Thomas Aquinas's *Summa theologiae*, which he completed only in 1520.[6] All these philosophical and theological enterprises will prove very useful twenty years later when he will have to debate a former monk called Martin Luther, an outcast of the Catholic church. According to Dennis Janz, the discussions between Cajetan and Luther are extremely important,[7] not only for the Catholic theology of the Roman church but also for the new Evangelical theology of the Lutherans.

Michael Tavuzzi shows that three years later, in 1501, Cajetan goes to Rome to take over the office of general procurator of the Dominican

---

2. Riva, *Analogia e Univocità in Tommaso de Vio "Gaetano"*, 26.
3. Martin, *Subverting Aristotle*, 138.
4. Finnis, *Natural Law and Natural Rights*, 185.
5. Grendler, *Universities of the Italian Renaissance*.
6. Clooney, *Theology after Vedanta*, 245n27.
7. Janz, *Luther and Late Medieval Thomism*, 124.

order,[8] in which capacity, according to tradition, he was supposed to preach before the pope and the cardinals in the first Sundays following Lent and the Pentecost. As we can see in Michael O'Connor, Cajetan performed most honorably in his new ecclesiastical position[9] by delivering a series of sermons which were anything but technical despite his exceptional theological and philosophical background. Furthermore, his sermons appear to avoid technicalities in general; in fact, they were as simple as possible regardless of whether his auditorium was made of the pope and the cardinals or simple folk.

In his sermons, Cajetan approached numerous subjects which were not only important but also practical, such as (1) the effectiveness of prayer, (2) the miracle of incarnation, (3) the cause and origin of evil, (4) the immortality of the soul, and (5) the reality of hell, which he approached, in the already traditional style of the Church of Rome, by focusing on the torments of the souls in hell. But he did so apparently to highlight the crucial importance of the immortality of the soul which, according to John Reilly, he defined as "a scientific truth."[10] Although they were as simple as possible, his sermons were based on Thomas Aquinas's extremely complex interpretations. Nevertheless, Cajetan somehow managed to turn them into simple and brief explanations which were easy to understand.

In 1507, Cajetan becomes vicar general of the Dominican order having been appointed in this office by the pope himself. A year later, in 1508, he climbs the order's hierarchy in becoming magister general, the highest position a Dominican monk could be appointed to. Benedict Ashley writes that Cajetan used his new office and its ecclesiastical importance to send missionaries to America,[11] some of which like Pedro de Cordoba, Antonio de Montécino and Bartolomé de las Casas were among the fiercest defenders of the rights of the native American populations.

Based on their missionary reports, Cajetan was able to include in his commentary on Thomas Aquinas's *Summa theologiae* a series of significant contributions about the immorality of the conquistadors who looted and plundered the lands of native American populations.[12] Even if the conquest policy of the new American territories was tacitly approved by the pope

---

8. Tavuzzi, *Prierias*, 92.

9. O'Connor, *Cajetan's Biblical Commentaries*, 20.

10. Reilly, *Cajetan's Notion of Existence*, 96.

11. Ashley, *Dominicans*, 139.

12. Adiele, *Popes, the Catholic Church*, 243.

himself, Cajetan defended the spiritual and ecclesiastical authority of the Roman bishop in the Catholic ecclesiology of the tempestuous sixteenth century alongside similar endeavors initiated by other Dominicans like Juan de Torquemada (1388–1468) in the fifteenth century and Robert Bellarmine (1542–1621) in the seventeenth century.

In his commentary on Thomas Aquinas's *Summa theologiae*, Cajetan defends the Thomistic doctrine of God's sovereignty over the universe and history. Thus, he points out that God's providence means more than foreknowledge; as shown by Luca Badini Confalonieri, his providence is in fact a sort of causality which allows God to move and influence all things "because Christ willed it to be so."[13] According to Cajetan, God's sovereignty presupposes that (1) history is continent and (2) the human being has free will. Extremely interested in the doctrine of sin and justification, Cajetan defends the teaching of original sin by confirming that sin cannot be avoided in the absence of God's grace.

Concerning justification, as evident in Christopher Malloy, Cajetan believes that grace is necessary in this respect,[14] but the justified believer can never be absolutely sure about his reconciliation with God. In other words, justification does not produce an absolute security about salvation even if, as Cajetan said, the human being must be preoccupied with Christian morality in everyday ecclesiastical, spiritual, and economic life. Erik Herrmann suggests that Cajetan's theology reflects the fundamental Catholic dilemma which cannot reconcile justification and sanctification since the justified believer is not sure about his salvation,[15] even if he is required to lead a moral life. Moreover, Cajetan discusses justification in the context of the Catholic Church's traditional claim to ecclesiastical and papal supremacy:

> Just as Abraham was accounted righteous because of faith and not because of his subsequent circumcision, similarly Peter received the keys because of his pontifical office over the Catholic Church and not because of the church of Rome or the subsequent pontifical office in Rome. Peter was given the keys when was made shepherd of the Christian fold. Just as the righteousness accounted in Abraham was not restricted to the time before circumcision but extended to the subsequent time of circumcision, in the same way

---

13. Badini Confalonieri, *Democracy in the Christian Church*, 116.
14. Malloy, *Engrafted into Christ*, 109n87.
15. Herrmann, "On the Babylonian Captivity of the Church (1520)," 67.

the keys Peter received extended to his subsequent pontifical office in Rome.[16]

One of Cajetan's most important contributions to the development of the Reformation were his discussions with Luther, which were held between 1518 and 1520. The two analyzed issues like indulgences, the confession of sins, and the authority of the pope, in which context Cajetan explained Luther what the *Exsurge Domine* bull entailed for Wittenberg's rogue theologian. If we are to believe Hans-Frederik Gustafson, the bull "represented a . . . defeat for Cajetan's moderate approach toward Luther."[17] Although he did not agree with Zwingli's 1525 perspective on the Lord's Supper or with Melanchthon's 1530 *Confessio augustana*, the very first Protestant confession of faith ever, Cajetan tried his best to find common aspects to both Catholic and Evangelical theologies. In this respect, Jared Wicks notices that "Cajetan did not brand Luther's teaching heretical,"[18] a key aspect which discloses the former's attitude to ecclesiastical doctrine.

Thus, Cajetan admitted that Catholics and Evangelicals (Lutheran and Reformed) could agree in at least four issues, such as (1) clerical marriage which could be accepted by the Catholic church, (2) the administration of the Lord's Supper with bread and wine (in Catholic churches it was administered only with bread), (3) the recognition of different ways to administer the Eucharist, and (4) personal liberty regarding ecclesiastical laws, which means that nobody should be forced to accept church laws without one's personal consent and conviction. All these could originate in what Phillip Cary calls "the medieval notion of theological certainty based on Scripture" which worked as "common ground for Luther and Cajetan and other Christian disputants of the sixteenth century."[19]

In soteriology, Cajetan distinguishes between faith in the revealed word of God and faith in the grace given to the human being in the current age. Also, he denies the Evangelical teaching that conferring meritorious value to good works diminishes the sufficient character of Christ's intercession because, as Malloy writes, in Cajetan there are "two justices, that of grace and that of works."[20] As far as Cajetan was concerned, the concept of merit refers to God's decision to reward believers as members in the body

---

16. de Vio Cajetan, *Cajetan Responds*, 137.
17. Gustafson, *Genesis of Cajetan's Exegesis*, 58.
18. Wicks, *Luther's Reform*, 175.
19. Cary, *Meaning of Protestant Theology*.
20. Malloy, *Engrafted into Christ*, 109n87.

of Christ. Thus, Cajetan points out that good works do confirm the value of Christ's work as head of the church, because in doing good works believers follow Christ's example.

Following in the footsteps of some of his Catholic colleagues with reforming ideas, Cajetan preferred the literal meaning of Scripture by avoiding cheap allegorizing and by correcting some of the Vulgate's mistakes. However, in doing so, Domenico Pietropaolo demonstrates that Cajetan was acutely aware of the role of metaphors in human language.[21] This attracted much criticism from his fellow Catholics even if, as we notice in Kenneth Hagen, Cajetan accepted Jerome's hermeneutics regarding the Old and New Testaments and read the latter through Erasmus's humanistic lens.[22] In the wake of his debates with Luther, however, Cajetan realized the importance of Scripture in defending Catholic faith and theology;[23] this is why he wrote commentaries to many biblical books such as the Psalms, the four Gospels, Pauline epistles, the general epistles, the Acts of the Apostles, the Pentateuch, the historical books from Joshua to Nehemiah, and Proverbs.

THOMAS MORE (1477–1535)

More was born in London into the family of a judge and had an exceptional education in the field of law studies which Peter Berglar argues "his father had imposed on him."[24] He studied theology on his own because he was deeply interested in the doctrines of the Christian religion and when the Reformation began in England he chose to side with the Catholics. This decision eventually led to his own death; More was executed,[25] because he defended the sovereignty of the Catholic church from the attempts of the royal dynasty to control the life of the church, as one can read in the history of Henry VIII and the house of Tudors.

A renowned humanist and classicist, More is famous for a book entitled *Utopia*,[26] in which he advances some proposals for the reformation of society based on ideas such as (1) a closed community, (2) common

21. Pietropaolo, *Semiotics of the Christian Imagination*, 65.
22. Hagen, *Hebrews Commenting from Erasmus to Beze*, 45.
23. Janz, *Luther and Late Medieval Thomism*, 156.
24. Berglar, *Thomas More*, 9.
25. Royer, *English Execution Narrative, 1200–1700*, 74.
26. More, *Utopia*.

property, (3) rigorously planned activities, (4) a ordered social life, (5) world values turned upside down (for instance, the night pot is made of gold), and (6) an austere life in general. Also, More defends humanist ideals, especially those suggested by Erasmus who, according to Eamon Duffy, wrote his *Praise of Folly* in More's house.[27]

Thus, More recommends the study of Greek in universities and churches, while criticizing scholastic theology. In his opinion, scholastic theology should be replaced by what he calls "positive theology," an epistemological enterprise based on rhetoric, not logic, as well as—Brian Gogan argues—"on induction from the sources rather than deduction from *a priori* principles according to the method of scholastic theology."[28] As far as More is concerned, Jesus's message was predominantly rhetorical and discursive,[29] not analytical and rationalistic. Christian theology should not be approached exclusively based on logic, sometimes used in excess, but must be preached to conquer the hearts of as many people as possible according to the model provided by the patristic homilies of the church fathers.

Following in Erasmus's footsteps, More carefully studied homiletics and patristic theology even if he focused mainly on Eastern patristic works to the detriment of their Western counterparts, so M. A. Screech informs us that he preferred the Greek fathers to the Latin.[30] More's works abound in quotations from Cyril of Alexandria, Gregory of Nyssa, and Gregory of Nazianz. Travis Curtright reminds us that More was a stern critic of the Continental reformers and especially of Luther's theology,[31] in which capacity he was not mild in his assessment of the Reformation. Concretely, he decries the fact that the Evangelicals gave up tradition as norm of theology which, at least in his view, denied not only Scripture's final authority, but also its dogmatic foundation. The early church, in his opinion, is crucial for a proper understanding of Scripture:

> my poor advice would be that in the study of holy Scripture one pay a special attention to the commentaries and other writings of early fathers of the Church. And also, that before agreeing with one or another of them, one before all else needs, along with grace and

27. Duffy, *Reformation Divided*, 45.
28. Gogan, *Common Corps of Christendom*, 2n3.
29. Paul, *Thomas More*, 8.
30. Screech, *Laughter at the Foot of the Cross*.
31. Curtright, *Thomas More*, 107.

> help from God (to be gotten with abstinence and prayer and clean living), to come good and solidly instructed in all the articles and points that the Church believes. These things once being firmly grasped and steadfastly, as undoubtable truths, presupposed, they and reason will then be two good guidelines by which to examine and expound all doubtful texts, since the reader can be sure that no text is to be understood in a way that goes against them both, or against any of the points of the Catholic faith of Christ's church.[32]

Also, More criticizes the Evangelical reformers' belief that the Catholic church were imbued with human traditions. On the contrary, More believes that the Catholic church is a divine institution which has a single faith based on the Holy Scriptures and defended by the writings of the church fathers and, as we see in Richard Marius, the sexual purity of the clergy.[33] Peter Marshall indicates that such criticism of Protestant theology can be found in his polemical writings, the most important of which is his *Confutation of Tyndale's Answer*.[34] More rejects Tyndale's conviction that Scripture can be understood without the interpretation provided by the church and the dogmatic tradition. According to More, Scripture is not sufficient for the understanding of the Christian message because divine revelation includes tradition by necessity.

In More's thought, the clarity and sufficiency of Scripture are two totally different issues because the human being can understand the biblical text, so he can grasp the content, but he cannot acquire the necessary meaning for salvation without the Holy Spirit's guidance of the clergy. Francis Gasquet demonstrates that More not only defended the clergy against Tyndale's criticism, but he did so fiercely.[35] In other words, Tyndale can understand the philology of the biblical text perfectly without having the full knowledge of saving faith. This polemical approach ended abruptly when More was arrested and incarcerated in the Tower of London. Awaiting execution, More wrote some devotional works[36] characterized by the sincerest spirituality which was somewhat lacking in his previous theological productions.

---

32. More, *Thomas More Source Book*, 274.
33. Marius, *Thomas More*, 517.
34. Marshall, *Beliefs and the Dead in Reformation England*, 58–59.
35. Gasquet, *Eve of the Reformation*, 75.
36. McCutcheon, "More's Rhetoric," 63–64.

Catholic Theology (1)

Contemplating his own death, More realizes and confesses that the only source of true comfort is trust in God's providence and goodness. Katherine Gardiner Rodgers reveals that, in More's last work, *Of Christ's Sorrow*, personal spirituality should be manifested through honest prayer and contemplative meditation according to the example provided by Christ in the Garden of Gethsemane.[37] A Catholic until death and a fervent supporter of the Church of Rome, More urges his readers to pray for and defend the true (Catholic) faith against those who supposedly waste God's grace (the Protestants). In concrete terms, (Catholic) believers are urged to partake in the Lord's Supper, approached obviously from a sacramental perspective, because—as Peter Ackroyd concedes—the Eucharist makes our conversation with God possible through prayer and meditation.[38]

ASSESSMENT QUESTIONS

1. What is Cajetan's opinion on God's sovereignty over creation?
2. What concessions did Cajetan do to reconcile with Evangelicals?
3. How does Cajetan define the role the concept of merit?
4. What does More's humanism entail?
5. How does More criticize Evangelical theology?

---

37. Gardiner Rodgers, "Lessons of Ghethsemane: De Tristitia Christi," 239.
38. Ackroyd, *Life of Thomas More*, 99.

11

Catholic Theology (2)
Ignatius of Loyola and Theresa d'Ávila

OBJECTIVES

1. To acquire essential knowledge about Loyola's life and activity;
2. To acknowledge the importance of the Society of Jesus or the Jesuit Order;
3. To become personally aware of how spiritual exercises work;
4. To understand the importance of conversion in the life of Theresa d'Ávila;
5. To know the mystical process of the union with Christ in d'Ávila's theology.

Key words: Ignatius, Theresa, spiritual exercises, mysticism, mission, prayer

IGNATIUS OF LOYOLA (1491–1556)

Founder of the Society of Jesus,[1] also known as the Jesuit Order and approved by the pope in 1540,[2] Ignatius of Loyola was not a theologian, at least not according to late medieval standards, because he wrote only one book, *Spiritual Exercises*, which is not a theological work but rather a

---

1. Sklar, *St. Ignatius of Loyola*.
2. Vande Kappelle, *New Creation*, 197.

Catholic Theology (2)

devotional booklet.³ Ignatius's theology, however, is presented not only in this production but also in his over seven thousand letters he sent all over the world after the year 1547.

Paschal Scotti shows that Ignatius was a special person because he did not become famous due to an exceptional university career like most of the reformers, both Catholic and Protestant. He also did not know Latin until the age of 33 when he learned it alongside students who could have been his own children. Three years after his conversion, in 1527, Ignatius began his academic studies at the University of Paris having decided to leave behind not only his military career but also his life as a *hidalgo*, with all the advantages of his being part of Spanish nobility.⁴

We find from Howard Kee that during his university studies which were completed with a bachelor's degree in 1533 and a master's degree in 1535, Ignatius brought together a cluster of students interested in missions. After only a few meetings, they all decide to go to the Holy Land to take the Christian faith to the Muslims in Palestine should God approve of their plans.⁵ Even if they needed the pope's approval and the founding of a missionary organization or a religious order was not exactly easy, they were all determined to turn the preaching of the gospel in Palestine the very purpose of their lives and careers, even if waiting for the pope's approval which came rather late was quite difficult.

Despite that the pope did not agree with their intended mission among the Muslims but ordered them to spread Catholic theology among the Protestants, Will Durant writes that the Society of Jesus managed eventually to send missionaries in the Americas, Japan, and China.⁶ Although they did not want it, the Jesuits' mission among the Protestants was more successful than the pope, Ignatius or his spiritual brothers had ever imagined because hundreds of years later, as Craig Atwood confirms, entire regions which used to be Evangelical in the sixteenth century, such as Poland, had turned back to Catholicism.⁷

Even if he never liked Lutheranism, Ignatius used to frequently read the writings of Lutheran theologians whom he never criticized in writing because he felt unfit for the task. Nevertheless, according to Thomas

---

3. Loyola, *Spiritual Exercises of St. Ignatius of Loyola*.
4. Scotti, *Galileo Revisited*, 66.
5. Kee, *Christianity*, 411.
6. Durant, *Complete Story of Civilization*, vol. 1.
7. Atwood, *Always Reforming*.

Hughes, he did encourage other Jesuits, like Diego Laynez and Peter Canisius,[8] to counter what they believed to be the Lutherans' dogmatic and practical errors. Almost totally uninterested in the important doctrinal debates of the first two sessions of the Council of Trent (1545–1547 and 1551–1552), Ignatius was nonetheless extremely pleased when three of his Jesuit colleagues were formally permitted to attend the council despite the general resentment against them.[9]

According to Joseph LaBelle, Ignatius advised the three—and all Jesuits for that matter—to express their point of view in humility,[10] preach as many times as they had the opportunity, teach the Scriptures, visit the poor and the sick, as well as think every night about how they could serve Christ's work at the council of Trento to the best of their abilities. The theological problems of the Catholic church, however, were never among Ignatius's main preoccupations because he always made time for practical and concrete issues. For instance, Ignatius went as far as to ask himself if it were not better for the Jesuits to withdraw from the debates held at the Council of Trent[11] to accept pastoral positions.

Nevertheless, Charles Polzer proves that all these questions and doubts originated in the fact that main interest of Ignatius and his Jesuit colleagues was the dissemination of the gospel among the pagans around the world,[12] not finding a solution to the theological controversies in Europe. In fact, Ignatius did not write or speak much about the doctrine of the Catholic church because—as we read in Robert Fitzgerald—he was convinced that it was not these which bring inner peace, but practical realities such as (1) prayer, (2) searching and finding God's will, as well as (3) pastoral work.[13]

For Ignatius, as we see in Joseph Conwell, the Society of Jesus was, or rather showed, a path to God,[14] so it is understandable why he focused on practical and ecclesiastical issues which he always attempted to solve by reading the four Gospels where he found details about Jesus's life and work. A firm promoter of practical theology, Robert Barth points out, Ignatius

---

8. Hughes, *Loyola and the Educational System of the Jesuits*.
9. McManamon, *Text and Contexts of Ignatius Loyola's "Autobiography"*, 88.
10. LaBelle, *From Strength to Strength*, 37.
11. Loyola, *Letters of St. Ignatius of Loyola*, 113.
12. Polzer, *Rules and Precepts of the Jesuit Missions of Northwestern New Spain*, 41.
13. Fitzgerald, *Soul of Sponsorship*.
14. Conwell, *Impelling Spirit*, 419.

wrote his *Spiritual Exercises* as a guide to every person's spiritual journey.[15] In his book, Ignatius presents the shift from conventional religious practice to full inner dedication which can help every person walk on the very path of Jesus. Thus, the purpose of the *Spiritual Exercises* is the Christian's total surrender to God's love and will.

The *Spiritual Exercises* are an introspective analysis of Ignatius's spirituality as they reflect his efforts to build a certain spiritual discipline for the everyday life of all Christians. Being fully aware that in its capacity as Christ's body, the church is made up of many limbs, each having its own different tasks, Ignatius managed to surround himself with people who excelled in the very fields where he lacked expertise. To give just one example, provided by William David Myers, he chose as personal secretary none other than Juan Alfonso de Polanco, a genuine expert in humanist sciences and Thomistic theology.[16]

Spiritually speaking, Ignatius tried his best to provide help for the soul as he was convinced that God works within every person's soul by guidance, teaching, and comfort. In this regard, Philip Sheldrake notices that Loyola offered advice on "how to teach spiritual discernment."[17] In dogmatic terms, as evident in Harvey Egan, this means that in his capacity as creator of all things, God is constantly in a direct connection with his creation, which is compelled to acknowledge God as Lord and creator.[18] Thus, every Christian, who must also be a servant of God, must always act according to his own spirituality and natural gifts which were bestowed upon him not only by creation but also by his becoming a member of the church. In other words, the Christian must give back to God what God gave him in the first place:

> I will call back into my memory the gifts I have received—my creation, redemption, and other gifts particular to myself. I will ponder with deep affection how much God our Lord has done for me, and how much he has given me of what he possesses, and consequently how he, the same Lord, desires to give me even his very self, in accordance with his divine design. Then I will reflect on myself and consider what I on my part ought in all reason and justice to offer and give to his Divine Majesty, namely, all

---

15. Barth, *Romanticism and Transcendence*, 96.
16. Myers, "Ignatius Loyola and Martin Luther," 142.
17. Sheldrake, "George Herbert and the Country Parson," 306.
18. Egan, *Ignatius Loyola the Mystic*, 97.

> my possessions, and myself along with them. I will speak as one making an offering with deep affection and say: "Take, Lord, and receive all my liberty, my memory, my understanding, and all my will—all that I have and possess. You, Lord, have given all that to me. I now give it back to you, O Lord. All of it is yours. Dispose of it according to your will. Give me your love and your grace, for that is enough for me.[19]

Thus, John O'Malley reveals that, according to Loyola, every Christian must work *spiritu, corde, practice*, namely in a very practical way, and from the bottom of his heart based on the Spirit's guidance wherever he may be.[20] Ignatius used to say that the world is our home,[21] so every Jesuit must be a missionary wherever he may be in the world. Every Jesuit had the duty to spread the gospel and preach the Christian faith especially among unbelievers. Nothing else matters and everything fades away by comparison to the preaching of the gospel in Ignatius who disapproved of medieval Catholic traditions such as prolonged fasting, penitence, and self-flagellation.

Knowing the case of Carlo Borromeo, the Catholic bishop of Milan,[22] who died of hunger at the age of 42 following prolonged fasting, Ignatius pointed out repeatedly that until they dedicate themselves fully to God, people like to do penance and treat their own bodies with unjustified harshness. Nevertheless, when they experience true conversion, they begin to reverently appreciate their bodies as God's gifts for them. Moreover, Ignatius was convinced that physical health was essential for the Christian mission as he frequently pointed out that the goal of the Jesuits was to work "in the Lord's vine" among those who do not know God.[23] This approach caused considerable irritation among some bishops because the Jesuits used to work among the pagans where the bishop's presence was non-existent and his authority extremely limited.

The *Spiritual Exercises*, however, were not aimed at the bishops, but at all the Christians who wished to live in a close relationship with Jesus. Thus, Ignatius insists on the contemplation of Jesus's life as if the believer were next to Jesus; this is why Ignatius urges his readers to image they walk with Jesus during his mission on earth. Each reader must imagine the

---

19. Loyola, *Ignatius of Loyola*, 176–77.
20. O'Malley, *Saints or Devils Incarnate?*, 107.
21. Donnelly, *Jesuit Writings of the Early Modern Period*, 157.
22. Bouley, *Pious Postmortems*, 54.
23. Curto, *Imperial Culture and Colonial Projects*, 406.

morning following the Last Supper and Jesus's sufferings in the Garden of Gethsemane. Everything must start with a prayer, then the reader will have to image Lord Jesus, our Lord, walking down Mount Sion where he had had supper with his disciples the night before. Having crossed Jerusalem and the valley between its walls, they arrive at the Garden of Gethsemane, at the foot of the Mount of Olives. Jesus calls three of his disciples, leaves them in a certain place, and then he goes a bit further away to be alone. He begins to pray so fervently that his sweat turns into blood. He prays three times in a row and three times he goes to wake up the three disciples who had fallen into deep sleep. After Judas came with the soldiers and gave him away by his treacherous kiss while Peter took the sword and cut off Malchus's ear, Jesus is apprehended like a criminal and taken to Anna's house. Ignatius insists that it is compulsory for us to imagine Mount Sion and the garden, its length and width; perhaps even how it looked like when these events happened. Then, we must ask ourselves what our heart's desire is and then we must learn to cry in love for the Lord Jesus's sufferings as well as pray that we also partake in them.[24]

THERESA D'ÁVILA (1515–1582)

Famous for her mystical preoccupations, Theresa is a second-generation Catholic reformer who showed a genuine passion for apologetic theology—the sort which, John Stackhouse tells us, exerts a powerful influence across the centuries.[25] As far as Theresa was concerned, every Christian believer must live in such a way that he is made aware of God's presence and its continuous manifestation. Born in a family of Jews who were forced to forge their documents to escape the Spanish Inquisition,[26] Theresa found it extremely difficult to study and write theology because the Inquisition had forbidden the reading of the Bible by lay people in 1554.

Antonio Pérez-Romero claims that another impediment was her scholarly training which did not include Latin.[27] Nevertheless, this did not prevent Theresa from either reading Scripture or studying theology. Thus, her entire work is ultimately a huge demonstration of courage. In Theresa's

---

24. Loyola, *Ignatius of Loyola*, 168–69.
25. Stackhouse, *Humble Apologetics*, 83.
26. Diaz, *Wrestling for My Jewish Identity*, 19.
27. Pérez-Romero, *Subversion and Liberation in the Writings of St. Teresa of Avila*, 97–98.

thought, Scott Hahn contends, the foundation of theology is Scripture,[28] which he uses metaphorically as invitation to seek a personal relationship with Jesus. Every Christian must read Scripture and evaluate his relationship with God through Jesus because it is through Jesus that we know God. Therefore, Theresa was very interested in exploring divine reality and existence.

Theresa used to say that everything begins with our personal and salvific relationship with Jesus or, as William Thompson-Uberuaga describes it, a "companioning process with Jesus."[29] She even confessed that she had converted following the contemplation of a statue representing Christ which helped her understand not only the importance of his humanity but also the greatness of his love for humanity. Impressed by Christ's suffering for sinners, Theresa understood that only God's grace can bring salvation even if the human being's answer is essential for the continuation of Christian life. Jess Hollenback writes that, in Teresa's theology, every Christian must go through a process of perfection,[30] which she compares to the cultivation and the tilling of a garden. This spiritual journey, however, must be always and permanently directed towards Jesus and his love for us:

> O, good Jesus! How clearly hast Thou shown that Thou art One with Him and that Thy will is His and His is Thine! How open a confession is this, my Lord! What is this love that Thou hast for us? ... I, at least, my Jesus, see clearly that Thou didst speak as a dearly beloved son both for Thyself and for us, and Thou hast such power that what Thou sayest in Heaven shall be done on earth. Blessed be Thou forever, my Lord, Who lovest so much to give that no obstacle can stay Thee.[31]

Convinced that the human being is capable of living in union with Christ despite original sin, Theresa defends the capacity of the human soul to receive divine grace by what Andreas Schmidt calls "continuous prayer."[32] She believed that prayer leads to a very close relationship with Christ despite the unbeliever's sin and lack of love. Anthony di Renzo underlines that, in Teresa, the believer's life must be an uninterrupted journey towards

---

28. Hahn, *Scripture Matters*, 182.
29. Thompson-Uberuaga, *Jesus and the Gospel Movement*, 20.
30. Hollenback, *Mysticism*, 505.
31. Avila, *St. Teresa of Avila "The Way of Perfection."*
32. Schmidt, *Remain in Me*, 6.

achieving "mystical union with Christ."[33] According to Teresa, union with Christ is essentially an epistemological process of growth into the knowledge of Christ through the activation of the will, reason, and feelings to achieve spiritual humility by acknowledging one's own limitations.

None of the human being's psychological faculties should be allowed to be a hinderance on the path of faith. When reason, for instance, no longer seeks spiritual truths it must be left in God's care, the only one who is able to perfect our spiritual journey towards union with Christ. As we see in Tomás Alvarez, this journey is essentially a mystical process at the end of which, as Theresa points out, the Christian will experience the mystery of the Holy Trinity by truly knowing Christ.[34] During the journey, however, while doing his best to follow in the footsteps of Jesus, the believer goes through a genuine ontological transformation,[35] which allows him to take one step at a time during this mystical path towards union with Christ.

ASSESSMENT QUESTIONS

1. What was Ignatius of Loyola's role in the various sessions of the Council of Trent?
2. According to Ignatius of Loyola's theology, which brings genuine inner peace?
3. What is the role of spiritual exercises in Ignatius of Loyola's theology?
4. What is the main characteristic of the Christian life in Theresa d'Ávila's theology?
5. What does the mystical journey towards union with Christ entail in Theresa d'Ávila's theology?

---

33. Di Renzo, *American Gargoyles*, 95.
34. Alvarez, *St. Teresa of Avila—100 Themes on Her Life and Work*, 443.
35. Dupré, "Unio Mystica," 10.

12

Radical Theology (1)
Andreas Bodenstein von Karlstadt and Thomas Müntzer

OBJECTIVES

1. To understand the most important aspects of Karlstadt's theology;
2. To figure out the reformations initiated by Karlstadt without Luther's support;
3. To comprehend the practical consequences of Karlstadt's theology;
4. To discern the connection between theology and social involvement in Müntzer;
5. To appreciate Müntzer's apocalyptic theology.

Key words: Karlstadt, Müntzer, sanctification, politics, righteousness, love

ANDREAS BODENSTEIN VON KARLSTADT (1486-1541)

One of the first radical reformers who rejected infant baptism and the co-operation between the church and the secular state, Karlstadt was also one of the first professors to be hired at the University of Wittenberg where

Radical Theology (1)

Luther activated throughout his theological career.[1] Holding degrees from the universities of Erfurt, Köln, and La Sapienza in Rome, where he obtained a doctorate in civil and canon law, Karlstadt decided to return to Wittenberg. When back home, Carter Lindberg discloses that Karlstadt became interested in Martin Luther's theology which he embraced only after a profound study of Augustine's theology.[2]

At first, Karlstadt was very supportive of Luther's reformation efforts as early as April 1517 when he published 152 Augustinian theses on nature, law, and grace. In the following two years, until 1519, Karlstadt taught theology based on Augustine's *De spiritu et litera* (On the Spirit and the Letter), then—as Volker Leppin tells us—he eventually gave up scholastic theology in favor of German mystical theology, especially the works of Johannes Tauler and Johann von Staupitz.[3] At the same time, as we read in Alejandro Zorzin, he taught Renaissance philosophy based on the works produced by Erasmus and Giovanni Picco della Mirandola.[4]

Also in 1519, Karlstadt decided to help Luther in his disputations with Johann von Eck from the University of Ingolstadt although, Carlos Eire informs us, it was von Eck who "baited Luther by arranging for a debate with Karlstadt at the University of Leipzig."[5] Eventually, as we read in Ronald Rittgers, von Eck decided to include him alongside Luther in the papal bull *Exsurge Domine*, with the proposition that he should be excommunicated from the Catholic church.[6] Karlstadt fought back and published an extremely acid pamphlet in which he provides details about how the pope himself is subject to error and sins, as well as how he can commit a whole range of unjust actions, one of which was evidently the excommunication of the two German theologians from Wittenberg.

Vincent Evener points out that following the 1521 Diet of Worms, when Luther's excommunication was confirmed officially but also during Luther's stay at the Wartburg Castle (May 1521-February 1522), Karlstadt worked alongside Melanchthon, Justus Jonas, Gabriel Zwilling, and Nikolaus von Amsdorf to initiate a program of reforms concerning (1) the

---

1. Hoogstraten, *Debaters*, 167.
2. Lindberg, *European Reformations*, 77.
3. Leppin, "Luther's Mystical Roots," 165.
4. Zorzin, "Andreas Bodenstein von Karlstadt," 327.
5. Eire, *Reformations*, 155.
6. Rittgers, *Reformation of Suffering*, 159.

Eucharist, (2) religious life, and (3) social life.[7] Consequently, in December 1521 and for the first time ever in Wittenberg, Karlstadt held a church service to celebrate the Eucharist according to the new Evangelical rite by using not only bread, as in the Catholic church, but also wine.

According to Lyndal Roper, on February 19, 1522, Karlstadt married Anna von Mochau,[8] and everything appeared to be back to normal when following Luther's return to Wittenberg the relationship between the two reformers began to deteriorate. Thus, a series of disagreements, especially dogmatic in nature, emerged rather rapidly between Karlstadt and Luther, while under Luther's influence, the University of Wittenberg censored Karlstadt's works until the formerly collegial connections between the two were damaged beyond repair. Consequently, Joel van Amberg reports that Karlstadt decided to move to the village of Orlamünde,[9] where he was forced to till the land in order no longer to depend on the salary provided by the Wittenberg church where he served as archdeacon.

Within only a few months, Karstadt became dramatically radicalized, he asked the peasants to call him "brother Andy," and formally renounced his doctoral titles, a decision Luther criticized in extremely harsh terms. In Orlamünde, Evener shows that Karlstand initiated a religious reformation[10] based on Luther's model which was nevertheless more conservative. Thus, Karlstadt's reformation included (1) a simple and even austere worship, (2) the administration of the Lord's Supper with bread and wine as remembrance of Christ's salvific death, (3) the removal of icons and statues from the church, (4) the postponing of infant baptism, (5) intense Bible study, and (6) the involvement of lay people in the church.

In 1524, Luther published a series of polemical writings against Thomas Müntzer (who had joined the peasants' revolt which eventually turned into a genuine war) and even if Müntzer did not have Karlstadt's support, Luther put them both in the same camp, a decision which infuriated Karlstadt who—according to Leppin—had to defend himself against this charge.[11] Because of these pamphlets and Luther's enormous influence among the German princes, Karlstadt was forced to leave Orlamünde following an order issued by prince Johann von Saxa. As of that moment, as

---

7. Evener, *Enemies of the Cross*, 163.
8. Roper, *Martin Luther*.
9. Van Amberg, *Real Presence*, 87.
10. Evener, "Andreas Bodenstein von Karlstadt," 80.
11. Leppin, *Martin Luther*.

we see in Amy Nelson Burnett, Karstadt decided to fight back and wrote a series of pamphlets against Luther (on infant baptism and the Lord's Supper) which he published in Basel.[12]

A few years later, in 1529, Karlstadt's financial situation worsened considerably. He contacted Zwingli who helped him work as deacon in Zürich and in 1534 he began to teach at the University of Basel. In 1541, Patrick Collinson indicates Karlstadt died of plague which he had contracted while he cared for the sick during that year's epidemic.[13] Thus, he fully demonstrated that his theological preoccupations (God's grace and justification by faith) were not empty words, but concrete actions.

Even if when he began his career Karlstadt was extremely preoccupied with the doctrine of justification which he considered anti-Pelagian, which—according to Ronald Sider—prompted even von Eck to check his discourse "to sound as anti-Pelagian as possible."[14] Later, Karlstadt became interested in sanctification as well as the impact produced by justification in the believer's life. Thus, Harry Loewen reveals that Karlstadt defended his doctrine of sanctification based on the *Epistle of James*,[15] which Luther saw as non-canonical. In Karlstadt's theology, the Christian acquires the true knowledge of God by faith and who has faith also has love for God, so he becomes God's friend. Such a person, Karlstadt points out, will accept God's will without reservation.

According to Sider, Karlstadt believed that the righteousness of the believer's heart must necessarily produce good works.[16] In Karlstadt, justification and sanctification are concerned with the believer's status not only before God but also before the people and the church. Thus, believers must never seek the help of secular authorities for dogmatic purposes; they must all study Scripture where they can find God's knowledge and will. Whoever does so will know how to live his life before God and the people. In other words, according to Karlstadt, believers must live sacrificially, like Christ himself:

> Christ's sacrifice is called obedience, body, blood, life, and the glory of his father. And in summary, Christ did God's will with the greatest diligence, more than all created beings, and more

12. Nelson Burnett, *Karlstadt and the Origins of the Eucharistic Controversy*, 54.
13. Collinson, *Reformation*.
14. Sider, *Andreas Bodenstein von Karlstadt*, 79.
15. Loewen, *Ink Against the Devil*, 35.
16. Sider, *Andreas Bodenstein von Karlstadt*, 134.

diligently than all angels and saints, more purely than his holy body, which is his holy church. And his obedience was his highest sacrifice, from which all other sacrifices in Christ receive their righteousness. For it was written of Christ in the beginning that he should do and become God's will, which he also perfected more than all other created beings could. Thus, sacrifices in heaven and earth, which the angels in heaven or the holy men on earth offer to God.[17]

Karlstadt underscored repeatedly that the pastor's duty is to focus the believers' attention on spiritual things alone, not on worldly and political events. He was extremely upset that Luther, as well as other reformers from Wittenberg or elsewhere, kept their pastoral offices while working with secular authorities. This is why, as we see in William Bouwsma, he decided to till the land like any other peasant,[18] a way of life that can be called Evangelical asceticism.[19] According to Karlstadt, this is what helps the pastor no longer to be dependent on the church's financial support.

Despite his false association with Müntzer, Karlstadt was firmly against the violence of the 1524–1525 peasants' revolt,[20] as he was convinced that neither Jesus nor his work needed any human help or at least not the violent kind. Christ commanded Peter to put down his sword, so all true Christians should do the same as followers of Christ. All those who put down their swords are members of the true church and follow the Lord by unceasingly taking up their cross and permanently staying close to the word of God which they can find in Scripture.

THOMAS MÜNTZER (1490–1525)

Even if not much is known about Müntzer's life, Ulrich Bubenheimer unveils the fact that following the completion of his university studies he was provost at the Benedictine cloister in Frose which he left after a while to study "true theology" in Wittenberg,[21] where the scandal of indulgences had already started. During his Wittenberg years, Müntzer saw himself as a follower of Luther although, as Gordon Rupp shows us, he felt attracted

---

17. Von Karlstadt, "On the Priesthood and Sacrifice of Christ," 93–94.
18. Bouwsma, "Anxiety and the Formation of Early Modern Europe," 226.
19. Zorzin, "Andreas Bodenstein von Karlstadt," 333.
20. Baylor, *Radical Reformation*, 266.
21. Bubenheimer, *Wittenberg 1517–1522*, 63.

more by Karlstadt's theology,[22] which aimed at a more profound reformation of civil society by detaching the church from the political influence of the secular state.

In 1519, Müntzer arrived in Zwickau,[23] where his sermons ignited a conflict with the Franciscan monks whose perspective on church hierarchy and traditional theology did not match his. Also, Müntzer despised the proverbial gluttony of the clergy and especially of the monks whose mouths he described as large enough to accommodate more than two kilograms of meat. According to Müntzer, however, the monks' main problem was not their extreme gluttony but the fact that they had forgotten not only Christ's way but also its corresponding suffering.

This conviction originates in his perspective on justification. Thus, John Oyer shows how Müntzer believed that God does not accept anybody anyhow but only those who follow Christ's commands through internal and external suffering, which is evidently personal.[24] This personal take on the doctrine of justification was almost surely fueled by Müntzer's expulsion from Zwickau after only a year since his arrival in the city. Thus, in 1523, he became a wanderer again only to reach the city of Allstedt where he decides to stay for as long as possible. While in Allstedt, Müntzer enjoyed a brief recess, during which time, as we are told by Eric Gritsch, he managed to write and publish some theological treatises.[25]

During his work in Allstedt, Müntzer began to preach against the German princes whom he considered ungodly and, quite obviously, bound to eternal damnation. Backed by the consistent support of his church in Allstedt, Müntzer continued his anti-government activities by refusing to pay taxes and by setting fire to a cloister's chapel as demonstration of the so-called "divine righteousness" which, as he said in his sermons, needed to serve the common folk. Andrew Pettegree believes that it is precisely this association with the common man that made Müntzer so appealing to the masses.[26] This is why Müntzer got in touch with some groups of rebel peasants whose leader he became, as he imagined, like Gideon himself.[27] Unfortunately, his spiritual and military leadership of the peasants put an

---

22. Rupp, *Patterns of Reformation*, 69.
23. Byrd, *Pentecostal Aspects of Early Sixteenth-Century Anabaptism*, 31.
24. Oyer, *Lutheran Reformers against Anabaptists*, 19.
25. Gritsch, *Thomas Müntzer*, 65.
26. Pettegree, *Reformation*, 1:337.
27. Williams, *Radical Reformation*, 163.

end to his life on May 27, 1525, when he and the people under his command were all executed following the quenching of the revolt by the joint armies of the German princes.

It is clear in Daniel Timmerman that Müntzer always had an apocalyptical theological perspective on history.[28] Thus, it was his deepest conviction that he had lived to see not only the end of times but also Christ's return to separate the elect from the damned. This fundamental conviction was based on an equally radical belief that Christianity's biggest problems was Augustine's doctrine of the church as *corpus permixtum*, namely a gathering which includes not only righteous people but also sinful persons. According to Andrew Bradstock, Müntzer was absolutely sure that he was one of the servants who wanted to pluck the tares off from the wheat,[29] according to the parable in Matthew 13. This radical and apocalyptical interpretation originates in his theology of creation; Müntzer believed that the entire creation was God's gift to the human being who was supposed to administer it and rule over it. The human being, however, decided to rebel against God and no longer listen to him even if his primordial duty was to serve God by ruling over creation. Those who believe, however, must live like Christ, not like Adam—they must suffer for the sake of Christ based on faith, not on their own works:

> suffering should be imputed to Christ alone, so that we need not suffer after Christ truly suffered for our sins. It should be noted here from what tenderness this improper tranquility is falsely presented to us. Adam is a model of Christ in a negative way, but Christ is the opposite. The disobedience of the creature is restored by the obedience of the word. The word was made flesh according to nature, like our carnal nature. Corresponding to the growth of faith, [the word] must partly diminish, just as happened to the whole Christ as the head. Thus, Christ atoned for the whole sin of Adam, so that the community would remain whole... The church suffers as his body. Paul was not able to suffer for the church except as a member who performs his duty. We must all follow in the footsteps of Christ, armed with such thoughts. In this respect, no gloss on Scripture can help those people who judge themselves

---

28. Timmerman, *Heinrich Bullinger on Prophecy and the Prophetic Office (1523–1538)*, 48.

29. Bradstock, *Faith in the Revolution*, 40.

superior, in their comfortable way, to those seeking righteousness through works.[30]

Consequently, because he put his trust only in creation and exclusively pursued wealth, power, and vain glory, the human being is no longer capable of seeing God who exists beyond it. According to Müntzer, man's rebellion had tragic consequences on the entire creation by the destruction of the relationship not only between the human being and the world, but also between him and his neighbor. The human being no longer rules the world but is ruled and seduced by the world; he no longer fears God but his neighbor (in Germany, the peasants feared the princes). Every Christian must truly fear God alone,[31] not other people, so the peasants must no longer fear the princes because God alone is their only true master (hence the idea to rebel against and annihilate the princes, seen as representatives of sin and evil).

In Müntzer's theology, as we see in Rittgers, the Christian's model is Christ,[32] who never allowed himself to be subject to the things of the world but chose to suffer unto death to provide Christians with an example which is not only spiritual, but also material. Thus, Müntzer believed that every Christian must go through a purification of the will which he calls purgatory. Travis Ables attests that, in Müntzer, Christians do not need a honey-sweet Christ, an allusion to forensic justification as proposed by Luther and Melanchthon,[33] but a bitter Christ who suffers enormously, like Müntzer himself.[34] Ultimately, the only way for the Christian to grow into likeness with Christ is suffering; as a matter of fact, as far as Müntzer is concerned, the life of a true Christian is nothing but suffering.

ASSESSMENT QUESTIONS

1. What kind of reforms did Karlstadt propose during Luther's stay in Wartburg?
2. What did Karlstadt's Evangelical Reformation consist of in Orlamünde?

---

30. Münzer, *Revelation and Revolution*, 83.
31. Chibi, *Fear God, Honor the King*.
32. Rittgers, *Reformation of Suffering*, 158.
33. Ables, *Body of the Cross*.
34. Loewen, *Ink Against the Devil*.

3. What does Karlstadt's doctrine of sanctification reside in?
4. What does Müntzer say about justification and sanctification?
5. What does Müntzer's Christology reveal about Christian life?

13

Radical Theology (2)
Caspar Schwenckfeld and Menno Simons

OBJECTIVES

1. To master the most important features of Schwenckfeld's theology;
2. To make sense of the relationship between will and faith in Schwenckfeld's theology;
3. To understand the teaching of following Christ in Schwenckfeld's theology;
4. To become familiar with the most important aspects of Menno Simmons's theology;
5. To be able to explain the relationship between faith and church in Menno Simmons's theology.

Key words: Schwenckfeld, Simons, holiness, celestial body, faith, will

CASPAR SCHWENCKFELD (1489–1561)

Although Schwenckfeld was born in a family of nobles and had pursued tertiary education, as we are told by Rufus Jones, he never got a bachelor, master, or doctoral degree.[1] Nevertheless, Schwenckfeld was an exceptionally gifted self-taught person whose writings reflect a deep knowledge of

---

1. Jones, *Spiritual Reformers in the 16th and 17th Centuries*, 65.

A Very Brief Introduction to Reformation Doctrine

classical literature, canon law, church history, and dogmatic theology. Having embraced the theses of Lutheranism since their first dissemination in 1517, Schwenckfeld remained what Elsie McKee calls a "lay theologian"[2] for his entire life; he was nonetheless a very competent intellectual and an expert in humanist writings, especially those of Erasmus.

Schwenckfeld did not stay long among the Lutherans because of his understanding of human will which, unlike Luther, he considered totally free and decisively active in man's salvation. At the same time, Bernard Reardon indicates that Schwenckfeld was not interested in the doctrine of justification which in Luther's theology focused mainly on the human being's legal status before God.[3] According to Edward Furcha, his foremost preoccupation was different, namely conversion or the new birth of the believer,[4] who—in his opinion—should let Scripture talk back to him. Thus, Scripture must never be adorned with human teachings, but should rather be listened to because of its divine teachings.

In Schwenckfeld's theology, Francesco Quatrini tells us, the duty of clergy, bishops, priests, and pastors, is to emphasize the importance of Scripture and allow it to unveil all the teachings of God without useless and false additions or even "restrictions."[5] As far as Schwenckfeld was concerned, the clergy did not fulfill its duty, which resulted in the dramatic decrease of ecclesiastical and social morality. The guilt of the clergy, especially Catholic clerics, consisted precisely in the fact that they did not do their best to teach the Holy Scripture to their believers in churches. As we see in Carter Lindberg, this is what caused Schwenckfeld to join the Evangelicals led by Luther, alongside whom he remained a most faithful adherent of the new theology until Luther's controversy with Erasmus.[6]

After 1525, when Luther unequivocally explained his perspective on the bondage of the will, Schwenckfeld refused to be called a Lutheran and insisted that he was only a mere Christian. As far as he was concerned, human will is far from being held captive by sin; on the contrary, human will is free to choose if it wants to be born again or not alongside the human being's entire nature. This explains why, according to Cyril O'Reagan, "Schwenckfeld abjures the doctrine of double predestination as

2. McKee, *Katharina Schütz Zell*, vol. 1, 455.
3. Reardon, *Religious Thought in the Reformation*.
4. Furcha, *Schwenckfeld's Concept of the New Man*, 43.
5. Quatrini, *Adam Boreel (1602–1665)*, 225.
6. Lindberg, *Third Reformation*, 103.

misrepresenting Christianity."[7] Schwenckfeld's soteriology focuses thus on the necessity of the human being's transformation through sanctification, not on the forgiveness of sins and sinful nature before God through justification. As we see in Abraham Friesen, "the future church," as he used to call whatever was supposed to emerge after Luther's reformation, namely the congregation of the sanctified and born again, will have to separate itself from "false Christians," or those who rely only on justification.[8]

Thus, in Schwenckfeld's theology, the will is in a close relationship with faith which he describes as the human being's desire to come closer to God through the knowledge and imitation of Jesus. As a matter of fact, in his theology, the believer not only desires but also merits God's grace—not through merit *per se* but, as Charles Byrd mentions, "through acts of piety enabled by the Holy Spirit."[9] In this respect, Schwenckfeld comes very close to Erasmus's theology and even to traditional Catholic theology. Faith presupposes the activation of the will, which can be seen in the believers' attempts to change his life through the transformation of his own sinful nature into a life of sanctification. Thus, Maximilian von Habsburg writes that Schwenckfeld's theology presupposed "an inward form of spirituality,"[10] which had to be expressed through pietistic efforts.

It must be underlined here that Schwenckfeld did agree with Luther that justification was appropriated by faith, but he insisted that true faith is always confirmed by the moral transformation of the sinful human being as well as by his desire to perform good works. This is in fact a reality which Alister McGrath calls "the moral regeneration of believers" in which "the believer is required to imitate Christ at the moral and spiritual levels, rather than merely to trust in God's promises."[11]

Thus, Schwenckfeld admitted that human nature was permanently and naturally inclined towards sin although, at the same time, it was essentially free and able to accept or reject the divine grace of salvation, especially because—as George Huntston Williams explains—"after regeneration the will is freed."[12] Apparently, Schwenckfeld was convinced that the freedom

---

7. O'Regan, *Gnostic Apocalypse*, 100.

8. Friesen, *Menno Simons*.

9. Byrd, *Pentecostal Aspects of Early Sixteenth-Century Anabaptism*, 41.

10. Von Habsburg, *Catholic and Protestant Translations of the Imitatio Christi, 1425–1650*, 149.

11. McGrath, *Reformation Thought*, 129.

12. Williams, *Radical Reformation*, 393.

A Very Brief Introduction to Reformation Doctrine

of the will is God's gift, so the possibility of activating human will with a view to accept salvation was an actual reality which generated good works. In Schwenckfeld, justification sanctifies to the point that there is no distinction between justification and sanctification; the believer is an entirely new person in Christ:

> This is . . . the true work of Christ and the office of his grace in the justification of the sinner, in that he . . . cleanses, renews, and sanctifies the natural man by the bath of the new birth and the renewing of the Holy Spirit, re-creating a new man or creature from an old man . . . This all takes places through Christ and his grace who leads us in the will of God to keep his commandments by his Spirit, and who desires to fulfill everything which might be lacking therein from his own satisfaction, if we continually cling to him by a true faith . . . Thus, our whole righteousness, as well as the new birth, grace, forgiveness of sins, merits, and all the treasures of heaven reach us in and through Christ, as also on his account.[13]

Paul Maier demonstrates that, as far as Schwenckfeld was concerned, good works did not possess any soteriological value in themselves, but faith cannot be authentic without them because doing good works is ultimately the work of God, not of man.[14] This means that Schwenckfeld did not agree with Luther's doctrine of passive justification because, as he pointed out, while Christ did open the way towards our salvation, we must also follow in his footsteps by taking up our own cross. If the human being really wants to "please Christ"—as André Séguenny puts it[15]—then he must take up his cross and follow Christ according to the teaching of Scripture.

As we see in Andrew Gamman, who sheds light on Schwenckfeld's "spiritualist emphasis,"[16] following Christ (in Schwenckfeld's theology) entails a series of key aspects, such as: (1) receiving or accepting Christ, (2) turn his life into our life, (3) live according to his teachings, and (4) endure his suffering and death. The cross does not forgive sins forensically, so Schwenckfeld did not believe that sins can be considered forgiven; the cross is a call to change and transformation, a call to the actual improvement of one's life. Furthermore, the cross confirms that sinful nature and

---

13. Schwenckfeld and Grater, "Commentary on the Augsburg Confession," 100–101.
14. Maier, *Caspar Schwenckfeld on the Person and Work of Christ*, 88.
15. Séguenny, *Christology of Caspar Schwenckfeld*, 55.
16. Gamman, *Church Invisible*.

death can be defeated. Consequently, as we see in Séguenny, Schwenckfeld's soteriology resembles that of Erasmus,[17] while his teaching about following Christ appears to imitate the entering the school of Christ which Erasmus presented so eloquently in his *Manual of the Christian Soldier*.

Since the believer is either holy or sinful, it is clear that the phrase *simul/semper justus et peccator* (simultaneously/always righteous and sinful) from Luther's theology was not exactly Schwenckfeld's favorite. To use Williams's words, "he would not tolerate the definition of the Christian as *simul justus et peccator*."[18] In this respect, he seems to have taken over the principle of classical Renaissance anthropology in which following Christ restores human dignity by allowing men and women to act individually. In Schwenckfeld's theology, the purpose of faith is a sinless human being.[19] Thus, he was convinced that while the necessity of divine grace remains a vital aspect of soteriology, it is the duty of the human being to take the first step towards his own salvation. In other words, everything depends on God when it comes to salvation although nothing can be achieved in the absence of human effort.

This dogmatic radicalism turned Schwenckfeld into a preferred target for Evangelicals while Catholics tried to seize him because of his doctrine of the Lord's Supper. In concrete terms, Schwenckfeld was convinced that the physical aspect of receiving the Eucharist (*manducatio oralis*, or the mastication of bread) had not soteriological significance; if anything at all really matters at the Lord's Supper than this is the faith of participants. Schwenckfeld abhorred the idea of *manducatio oralis* because he must have seen it as an ecclesiastical ceremony and John Rempel clearly shows that, in Schwenckfeld, "ceremonies stand in the way of God's communication with us."[20]

Regarding Christ's presence in the elements of the Lord's Supper, namely in bread and wine, Aarne Ruben proves that Schwenckfeld insisted on Christ's body being the same on earth and in heaven,[21] unlike Luther who believed that the body of the glorified Christ, after his resurrection, was different from the body he had prior to resurrection. Consequently, it appears that Schwenckfeld was convinced that Christ's body was equally

17. Séguenny, "Caspar von Schwenckfeld," 358.
18. Williams, *Radical Reformation*, 204.
19. Séguenny, "Caspar von Schwenckfeld," 353.
20. Rempel, *Lord's Supper in Anabaptism*, 132.
21. Ruben, *Story of Lutheran Sects*, 79.

spiritual and physical which meant that it was impossible to represent it artistically by means of images or statues.

The mystery of Christ's spiritual body is profoundly ineffable, so the only thing we can do is just talk about it without attempting to represent it in any way whatsoever. This is the reason behind Schwenckfeld's stance against the physical aspects of the Lord's Supper; in this respect, Amy Nelson Burnett writes that "Schwenckfeld warned against leading Christians astray from the one, spiritual eating of Christ's body to a different, physical eating of his body."[22]

Due to the spirituality of his body, Christ is simultaneously a human being and the New Human Being whose celestial body neither destroys nor absorbs human nature because, as Stephen Webb clarifies, "a celestial body for Schwenckfeld is a moral achievement, one which we can too gain in the afterlife."[23] Thus, in Schwenckfeld's thought, the New Human Being is a genuine human being within a divine celestial being. Christ's celestial body is accessible and available at the Lord's Supper but only by faith.

As a Protestant, Schwenckfeld insists that his entire Christology can be found in Scripture. Unlike Luther, however, who believed that Scripture was the only source of faith and the promise of the forgiveness of sins, Schwenckfeld explains that Scripture opens our horizon to the things promised by faith as God's gift. In Schwenckfeld's theology therefore, Scripture is not the source of faith, but only a guide for the human being in search of faith; a guide which, Gerrit Voogt tells us, works like a "mirror" and an "arena" for the believer's "knowledge and faith."[24]

MENNO SIMONS (1496-1561)

Menno was probably the most famous of the moderate radical reformers,[25] also known as Anabaptists, because they used to baptize again all those who wished to join them even if they had been baptized in the Catholic church. As far as we know, it seems that Menno worked almost his entire life in the region of the city of Köln, where he participated in many theological controversies with Albert Hardenberg, a well-known Reformed divine from Bremen. Even if the lacked university studies, an aspect Hardenberg

---

22. Nelson Burnett, *Karlstadt and the Origins of the Eucharistic Controversy*, 131.
23. Webb, *Jesus Christ, Eternal God*, 155.
24. Voogt, *Constraint on Trial*, 59.
25. Buckwalter Horst, "Menno Simons: The Road to a Voluntary Church," 197.

disclosed to Melanchthon, Wim Janse tells us[26]—Menno was ordained priest at the age of 28 because of his good knowledge of Scripture and Erasmian philosophy. Following his conversion to Protestantism, Menno was always on the run because Protestant and Catholic authorities in Germany and the Low Countries never ceased to hunt him. According to what we see in Abraham Friesen, his conversion to Protestantism, however, seems to have never separated him from Erasmus's theology.[27]

Thus, Abraham Toews divulges that Menno's theology seems to have a number of Erasmian features,[28] the most important of which are the following: (1) a focus on the power and freedom of human will (the will is always stronger than reason or intellect), (2) a moral interpretation of the Bible, (3) the firm dichotomy between body and soul, (4) an evident preoccupation for style (in speech and writing) as an effective way to present the gospel, (5) the conviction that some godly pagans were moral examples worthy of imitation. To a rather large extent, Menno's activity was a genuine exercise in the preaching of the gospel whose foundation is the living and sanctifying word of the gospel of Jesus Christ. Cornelius Dyck explains that, in Menno, the preaching of the gospel is so important because it originates in God's promise, in God's word.[29]

Menno's theology is founded on Scripture as source of ecclesiastical reformation and his reforming efforts always aimed at the making Scripture available to all earnest Christians. For instance, William Estep writes that Menno displayed a "wide knowledge of the Bible."[30] No wonder the Dutch radical reformer insisted that true Christians are those who not only know God's word from Scripture, but also have Christ's Spirit like the apostles. Menno always wanted to have in his church only Christians who think like Christ; as we see in Jacob Loewen and Wesley Prieb, these are the true Christians, namely those who are born again through the hearing of God's word from Scripture and who, having become new beings following conversion, wish to live in subjection to Christ and want to do good works as demonstration that they lives were changed by the Holy Spirit of God.[31]

---

26. Janse, *Albert Hardenberg als Theologe*, 353.
27. Friesen, "Erasmus," 469.
28. Toews, *Problem of Mennonite Ethics*, 111–12.
29. Dyck, *Introduction to Mennonite History*.
30. Estep, *Anabaptist Story*, 170.
31. Loewen and Prieb, *Only the Sword of the Spirit*, 190.

A Very Brief Introduction to Reformation Doctrine

Leonard Friesen exposes Menno's thought as characterized by an acute sense of urgency.[32] Thus, the gospel must be preached persistently because Christ's return is near, which means that the essence of his theology is conversion followed by sanctification. The new birth is vital for every Christian because, as Menno explains, grace, the forgiveness of sins, and Christ's virtues are offered to every believer only after he was born again through faith. According to Lawum Kayamba, in Menno, faith produces fear of God, while this is what differentiates between those who are saved and those who are condemned to eternal death.[33]

Paul Hinlicky correctly notices that, in Menno, "faith is the source of all true virtue" because "the heart of faith is obedience to a divine demand."[34] According to Menno, true faith is (1) trust in the forgiveness of sins, (2) the fruit of righteousness, namely good words, (3) the desire to apply righteousness in practice, (4) the eradication of fallen human nature, (5) the crucifying of pleasures and forbidden desires, (6) the glorification of the cross of Christ, (7) spiritual renewal, (8) the new birth, and (9) the believer's spiritual (not physical) resurrection in Christ. Also, faith is God's gift and the power given by God to believers for an active living characterized by morality and good works. As Timothy George puts it, "the believer, moved by an unfeigned faith, was able to love God, returning love for love," like Abraham and Moses.[35] Menno believes that through faith, every Christian acknowledges that not only the gospel but also the law is righteous and true. Thus, the believer must strive for perfection, the sort which is anchored in Christ:

> for Christ's sake we are in grace, for his sake we are heard, and for his sake our failings and transgressions, which are committed involuntarily, are remitted. For it is he who stands between his Father and his imperfect children, with his perfect righteousness and with his innocent blood and death, and intercedes for all those who believe on him and who strive by faith in the divine word, to turn from evil, follow that which is good and who sincerely desire . . . that they may attain the perfection which is in Christ . . . We do not believe, nor teach that we are to be saved by our merits and works . . . but that we are to be saved solely by grace, through

---

32. Friesen, *Mennonites in the Russian Empire and the Soviet Union*.
33. Kayamba, *Social and Political Dimension of the Kingdom of God in Mark*.
34. Hinlicky, *Beloved Community*, 265.
35. George, *Theology of the Reformers*, 281.

Christ Jesus . . . By grace was man created, through Christ Jesus. By grace he was again accepted through Christ when he was lost.[36]

Sjouka Voolstra shows us that, in Menno, faith is ultimately the believer's willful subjection to the gospel, which is considered Christ's new law and the very foundation of the church.[37] In Menno's theology, as highlighted by Veli-Matti Kärkkäinen, the church has the following characteristics: (1) a biblical doctrine which cannot be falsified by theologians, (2) the administration of baptism and the Lord's Supper only to those who truly repented of their sins, so only to those who became born again or converted, (3) obedience to true faith, not cheap grace, (4) brotherly love, (5) the confession of Christ, and (6) the ardent desire to suffer for the true faith in Christ.[38]

Consequently, divine grace cannot be mediated by the sacraments, but only by God's word in a church of genuine saints. Unlike Augustine and Luther, as McGrath points out, Menno believed that the church was not a *corpus permixtum*, but the gathering of those who truly repented of their sins which means that the true church is characterized by the implementation of strict discipline.[39] According to Menno, the necessity of ecclesiastical discipline originates in the fact that the final authority of the church is Christ himself or, as Dave Andrews writes, "Christ was the cornerstone of the true church."[40] This is why all genuine Christians must faithfully follow the example of Christ which can be found on the pages of the Holy Scripture.

ASSESSMENT QUESTIONS

1. What is the connection between faith and sanctification in Schwenckfeld's theology?
2. What does following Christ entail in Schwenckfeld's theology?
3. What are the implications of Schwenckfeld's belief in Christ's celestial body?

---

36. Simons, *Complete Works of Menno Simons*, 263.
37. Voolstra, "Menno Simons," 369.
38. Kärkkäinen, *Hope and Community*, 302.
39. McGrath, *Christian Theology*, 157.
40. Andrews, *People of Compassion*, 37.

4. What is the definition of true Christians in Menno Simmons's theology?

5. What does true faith imply in Menno Simmons's thought?

14

Conclusion

The Impact of Reformation Theology

OBJECTIVES

1. To acquire a general knowledge of the most important Christian doctrines influenced by Reformation theology;

2. To become familiar with the most important intellectual, social, and cultural domains influenced by Reformation theology;

3. To be aware of some of the modern and contemporary theologians influenced by Reformation theology;

4. To understand the importance Reformation theology had for the relationship between worship and spirituality;

5. To comprehend the importance Reformation theology had for the relationship between ethics and eschatology.

Key words: Reformation, impact, pietism, liberalism, Scripture, society

REFORMATION THEOLOGY HAD A series of notable consequences on the historical evolution of Christianity not only from a doctrinal or dogmatic point of view, but also from a practical one. The first and probably the most important consequence of Reformation theology is most likely confessionalization, as we see in Erika Rummel's excellent study of this religious phenomenon,[1] namely the emergence of new Christian confessions/churches of Evangelical persuasion based on a certain confession of faith which provided detailed explanations regarding the theological convictions of those churches. Likewise, Donald Fairbairn and Ryan Reeves explain that the confessions of faith were intended to differentiate that church from other Protestant churches with different doctrinal convictions, even if only in matters of trivial dogmatic importance.[2]

The second vitally important consequence of Reformation theology for the history of the Christian church was, as revealed by Sasja Mathiasen Stopa,[3] the dialectics between law and gospel. This vital aspect was coupled with the doctrine of justification by faith alone—John Fesko wrote a masterful book about it[4]—which influenced not only traditional Protestantism (in the sense that all Protestant confessions, Lutheran, Reformed, and even Radical acknowledged its key role for faith and practice) but also liberal Protestantism, Brian Gerrish tells us,[5] which used it to develop the theoretical foundations of the correlation method.[6] According to Leslie Murray, one of the liberal theologians who used this method was Paul Tillich.[7] Tillich writes that justification presupposes a reality contrary to a factual situation, such as the human being who is justified by grace through faith even if he does not deserve to be accepted by God, so—as we read in Charles Amarkwei—correlation implies the juxtaposition of two irreconcilable or paradoxical facts.[8]

Within the same liberal Protestantism, Leif Svensson shows that Ludwig Feuerbach, one of the first Hegelian theologians, used Luther's conviction that faith makes God to promote the so-called projection theory,[9] namely that God is a projection of human reason or of the human psyche's extremely subjective character which works based on a series of complex rational processes. Before him, Timothy Luther advocates the idea that Hegel himself acknowledged the decisive impact exerted by the

---

1. Rummel, *Confessionalization of Humanism in Reformation Germany*.
2. Fairbairn and Reeves, *Story of Creeds and Confessions*.
3. Mathiasen Stopa, *Soli Deo Honor et Gloria*.
4. Fesko, *What Is Justification by Faith Alone?*.
5. Gerrish, *Old Protestantism and the New*.
6. McGrath, *Historical Theology*, 194.
7. Muray, *Liberal Protestantism and Science*, 73.
8. Amarkwei, *Paul Tillich and His System of Paradoxical Correlation*, 136.
9. Svensson, *Theology for the Bildungsbürgertum*.

Conclusion

Reformation,[10] in all its Protestant branches, on the development of the concept of subjectivity.[11]

The Reformation as a whole, namely both its magisterial confessions (Lutheran and Reformed churches which supported the cooperation between church and state) and its radical branches (especially Anabaptism which rejected any connections between church and state), profoundly influenced Dietrich Bonhoeffer.[12] Michael DeJonge lets us know that, on the one hand Bonhoeffer supported the application of the notion of *adiaphora* (unimportant things which the church should most likely disregard, such as ecclesiastical vestments, in order to avoid controversy), while on the other hand actively stood against secular authorities by refusing to accept the national socialism of the Nazi Party in Germany, during the tumultuous interwar period of the 1930s and 1940s.[13]

If we read Kimlyn Bender, we understand that Karl Barth's entire theology reflects the importance of the external character of God's word (*extra nos*) as present in the theology of the Magisterial Reformation promoted especially by Luther, Melanchthon, and Calvin.[14] As such, the reality of God's word remains permanently external to believers in the sense that the Bible becomes God's word through the work of the Holy Spirit who illuminates the reader's mind and helps him understand it. Understanding Scripture, however, is only one side of theological reality; the other one, Carter Lindberg suggests, is its practical application through a holy life as underlined mainly by Karlstadt whose theology laid the basis of the Pietist movement successfully represented by Johann Arndt and Philip Jakob Spener in the seventeenth century.[15] Karlstadt's intention to take the reformation of the church beyond Luther's achievements inspired the Pietist theologians who strove not only to preserve the correct understanding of doctrines but also to apply them practically by means of concrete actions such as the establishment of hospitals, orphanages, and hospices for the elderly. These endeavors were enacted as proof of personal and communitarian holiness based on what Christopher Barnett describes as an "ethic of love."[16]

10. Luther, *Hegel's Critique of Modernity*, 89.
11. James, *Hegel's Philosophy of Right*.
12. Mauldin, *Barth, Bonhoeffer, and Modern Politics*, 69.
13. DeJonge, *Bonhoeffer on Resistance*, 91–95.
14. Bender, *Reflections on Reformational Theology*.
15. Lindberg, *Third Reformation*, 142.
16. Barnett, *Kierkegaard, Pietism, and Holiness*, 114.

A Very Brief Introduction to Reformation Doctrine

Reformation theology also led to the emergence of Methodist theology, Roy Long tells us;[17] thus, John Wesley used to commend Luther for his efforts to read Scripture which helped him discover the doctrine of justification, even if the same Wesley decried the fact that Luther did not fully understand the doctrine of sanctification based on concrete actions,[18] such as the separation between church and state as well as the rejection of any form of violence. These practical aspects, however, were promoted not only by Menno Simons's Anabaptist Protestantism,[19] but also by Ignatius of Loyola's Mystical Catholicism,[20] whose theologies influenced the modern world in rejecting the cooperation between church and state as well as the corresponding violence that originates from such a connection.

The third extremely important consequence of Reformation theology is its impact on hermeneutics, as David Baronov claims in his study about research methods.[21] For instance, Jens Zimmerman argues that Flacius's main work, the *Clavis sacrae Scripturae*, can be considered the first book of modern hermeneutics,[22] while the intense Bible studies like those organized by Zwingli and his students, coupled with the humanists' interest in biblical philology, led to the emergence of numerous organizations and societies focused on the translation of the Bible in various world languages, a reality Bruce Metzger investigates in detail.[23] Likewise, Claude Welch maintains that this special interest in Scripture led to the development of variegated historical-critical studies, so specific to liberal and rationalistic Protestantism represented by Ferdinand Christian Baur, Albrecht Ritschl, and Adolf von Harnack among many others.[24]

Then, the Protestants' interest in the study of Patristic theology, promoted mainly by Melanchthon,[25] resulted in a special preoccupation for the relationship between the early church and the modern church. Thus, one can speak of a radical redefinition of Christian ecclesiology based on

---

17. Long, *Martin Luther and His Legacy*.
18. Lewis, *Anti-Methodism and Theological Controversy in Eighteenth-Century England*, 65.
19. Varkey, *Role of the Holy Spirit in Protestant Systematic Theology*, 62.
20. Lodyzhenskii, *Light Invisible*.
21. Baronov, *Conceptual Foundations of Social Research Methods*.
22. Zimmermann, *Recovering Theological Hermeneutics*, 82.
23. Metzger, *Bible in Translation*, 9–10.
24. Welch, *Protestant Thought in the Nineteenth Century*, 2:176.
25. Meijering, *Melanchthon and Patristic Thought*.

Conclusion

the concept of the dogmatic succession of believers or, as Aza Goudriaan terms it, "the succession of doctrine,"[26] not on the traditional and historical succession of bishops as in Catholic theology. In other words, by stressing the relationship between the believer and Christ, Reformation theology inspired a genuine theology of God's presence throughout the whole Protestant tradition from the sixteenth century to contemporary times.

Reformation theology is even more important considering that all the sixteenth-century theologians, both Protestant and Catholic, were interested first and foremost in Christ's work and the dissemination of Christ's gospel, which means—as Peter Kreeft put it—that we can learn from each other.[27] Consequently, Reformation theology was not only an academic exercise (even if it started as a pastoral event caused by a series of problems specific to church life and debated by university professors), but also an effort rooted in the practical reality of the local churches and society in general. In this respect, David Larsen states, somewhat condescendingly, that Reformation theology (associated with what he calls "the coming of age of preaching") led to the rediscovery of biblical preaching and pastoral theology (compared to the Middle Ages, which Larsen dubs "the adolescence of preaching").[28] This homiletic focus on the Bible was possible because Reformation theologians were not primarily interested in scientific objectivity but in the preaching of the gospel so that it should be understood by common folk.

The Reformation always underscored the actuality of Scripture because the Bible was not seen as a collection of old and irrelevant books; on the contrary, Scott Manetsch states that it was considered God's fully inspired word,[29] which works powerfully in any age, in any moment of history, regardless of the human perceptions of it. Thus, even if they were extremely preoccupied with the translation of the Bible in national languages, Protestant theologians were not interested in philology alone, namely exclusively in translations, but also in the content of Scripture; in most cases, the Bible translators were also preachers and the preachers were Bible translators, as one can see in the lives of Luther and Tyndale.[30]

---

26. Goudriaan, "Reformed Theology and the Church Fathers," 14.
27. Kreeft, *Catholics and Protestants*.
28. Larsen, *Company of the Preachers*.
29. Manetsch, "'I Have the Word of God,'" 25.
30. Delisle and Woodsworth, *Translators through History*, 167.

A Very Brief Introduction to Reformation Doctrine

Despite various schisms and misunderstandings within the Protestant camp, such as the Lutherans refusing to work with Zwinglians, Zwinglians with Anabaptists, and Anabaptists with Lutherans, Bernd Oberdorfer supports the idea that the fundamental feature of Reformation theology is the focus on spreading the gospel so that God should be known not only in the church, but also in society.[31] Thus, even if most reformers did officially belong to this or that church, in the sense that they were Lutherans, Zwinglians, Calvinists, or Anabaptists, some theologians (especially lay persons) rejected any pigeonholing attempt; for instance, Argula von Grumbach and Katharina Schütz Zell constantly fought for peace and understanding among all Protestants, but also between Protestants and Catholics.

It is extremely important to remember that the Reformation began as an attempt to change the church's doctrine and practice because of some very serious mistakes, although—as Erwin Iserloh convincingly demonstrates—the Reformers never intended to establish a new church, or more churches, as it happened eventually.[32] On the contrary, they strove to reform the extant one, the Catholic church. In this context, Lutheran theology came because of a series of debates within the Catholic church which harbored numerous theologians with reforming ideas, like Erasmus and the humanists. Unfortunately, as one can see in John Maxfield, the excommunication of Luther and the first Evangelical theologians from the Catholic church led not only to dogmatic confessionalization but also to a permanent ecclesiastical separation.[33]

Despite these schismatic movements, Reformation theology's main and final purpose, both in Protestant and Catholic contexts, was to provide a solution to the problem of sin and to explain the reality of the human being's salvation by God based on the teachings of Scripture, seen as God's inspired word and the quintessence of objective truth. Thus, the contribution of Reformation theology is visible in all the fields of Christian doctrine and practice since the two (*fides* and *praxis*) are always inseparable.[34] This is why most of the Protestant and Catholic theologians with genuine preoccupations in the reformation of church life wrote catechisms both for adults and children to help them learn the doctrines of Scripture more easily.

---

31. Oberdorfer, "Law and Gospel and Two Realms," 33.

32. Iserloh, "Development of Denominations in the Sixteenth and Seventeenth Centuries," 420.

33. Maxfield, *Luther's Lectures on Genesis*, 2.

34. Ptaszynski and Bem, *Searching for Compromise?*, 286.

Conclusion

Finally, the most dogmatic of their writings contain numerous applications even if the latter appear to be always the natural consequence of the former.

Timothy George provides an excellent synthesis of the wide range of dogmatic issues which stemmed from the Reformation as a religious movement. According to George, Reformation theology had an overwhelming impact on some essential dogmatic and practical aspects of the church and Christian life,[35] of which the most important are the following: (1) the doctrine of God as Holy Trinity which primarily underlines God's sovereignty manifested in predestination by the election of some to salvation (or eternal damnation, even if this aspect was elegantly avoided both in dogmatic treatises and in sermons),[36] (2) the doctrine of Christ which emphasizes Christ's work for the salvation of humankind, but not as much his person which was considered a closed issue since the time of the early church,[37] (3) worship and spirituality which, among the Protestants, brought to light the importance of the preaching of Scripture as God's fully inspired word and source of the doctrines of justification by faith alone and sanctification by good works generated by the corresponding reality of justification,[38] (4) Scripture and ecclesiology which underline the necessity of the constant reading of Scripture to know God, the fellowship or communion between believers and God, as well as the fellowship among believers as brothers and sisters since the church is defined as the gathering or the elect, sanctified and preserved by God in grace,[39] and (5) ethics and eschatology which are based on the conviction that Evangelical morality, deeply rooted in Scripture, must face and confront secular culture in attempting to transform it through the word of God;[40] thus, Evangelical ethics must never be subject to secular culture because it must always be approached from the perspective of eschatology that constantly insists on Christ's return.

To conclude, Reformation theology—especially that of a radical, Anabaptist sort, preaching, and ethics are characterized by an obvious "eschatological urgency," a phrase which appears to have been coined by George Huntston Williams in his famous study about the Radical Reformation.[41]

35. George, *Theology of the Reformers*, 308ff.
36. Kaiser, *Doctrine of God*, 110–18.
37. Franks, *History of the Doctrine of the Work of Christ*, 317ff.
38. Campi, "Was the Reformation a German Event?," 24.
39. Kärkkäinen, *Introduction to Ecclesiology*.
40. Barnes, "Eschatology, Apocalypticism, and the Antichrist," 233.
41. Williams, *Radical Reformation*, 277.

A Very Brief Introduction to Reformation Doctrine

Thus, the theologians of the Reformation, both Protestant and Catholic, were convinced that all Christians must not only preach the teachings of Scripture by word and deed, but also live them out in the practice of everyday life because the return of Christ, the Lord of the church, is a matter of absolute certainty. In other words, the message of Reformation theology is this: we must always live for Christ while being fully convinced that—as Joel Beeke compellingly asserts[42]—one day we shall see him face to face; we shall see him who is not only our salvation and future, but also our joy and life itself.

Across the entire spectrum of Reformation theology, everything depends on Christ and points to Christ, but his truth must never be preserved only for the benefit of the Christian community. On the contrary, it must be preached to everybody, hoping that those who do not know Christ will eventually come not only to know about him but also to really know him and receive him in their lives as Lord and Savior.[43] In doing so, they are supposed to become members of the church and enjoy eternal life which beings now, in our lifetimes. Thus, Reformation theology is based on the conviction—so powerfully expressed by Karl Barth—that Christ alone is our hope[44] and, by extension, the hope of the entire world. Also, the preaching of God's word in the world must be done boldly, faithfully, and convincingly because we know that Jesus conquered the world and we, as his disciples and followers, are more than conquerors (Rom 8:37) in all respects, according to the testimony of the Holy Scripture.

ASSESSMENT QUESTIONS

1. What was the impact of Reformation theology on Hegel and Feuerbach?
2. How did Karlstadt's Reformation theology influence the Pietist movement?
3. How was modern hermeneutics influenced by Flacius's thought?
4. Which Christian doctrines were especially influenced by Reformation theology?
5. What was the impact of Reformation theology on eschatology?

---

42. Beeke, *Revelation*.
43. Noll and Nystrom, *Is the Reformation Over?*, 89.
44. Barth, *Knowledge of God and the Service of God*, 100.

Bibliography

Ables, Travis E. *The Body of the Cross: Holy Victims and the Invention of the Atonement.* New York: Fordham University Press, 2021.
Ackroyd, Peter. *The Life of Thomas More.* New York: Anchor, 1999.
Adiele, Pius O. *The Popes, the Catholic Church and the Transatlantic Enslavement of Black Africans 1418-1839.* Hildesheim: Olms, 2017.
Althaus, Horst. *Hegel: An Intellectual Biography.* Cambridge: Polity, 2016.
Alvarez, Tomas. *St. Teresa of Avila—100 Themes on Her Life and Work.* Washington, DC: Institute of Carmelite Studies, 2011.
Amarkwei, Charles. *Paul Tillich and His System of Paradoxical Correlation: Forging a New Way for Science and Theology Relations.* Eugene, OR: Wipf & Stock, 2020.
Amberg, Joel van. *A Real Presence: Religious and Social Dynamics of the Eucharistic Conflicts in Early Modern Augsburg 1520-1530.* Studies in the History of Christian Traditions 158. Leiden: Brill, 2011.
Andersen, Ragnar. *Concordia Ecclesiae: An Inquiry into Tension and Coherence in Philipp Melanchthon's Theology and Efforts for Ecclesiastical Unity, Especially in 1527-1530.* Zurich: Lit, 2016.
Andrews, Dave. *People of Compassion.* 2008. Reprint, Eugene, OR: Wipf & Stock, 2012.
Arnold, Jonathan. *The Great Humanists: An Introduction.* London: Bloomsbury, 2011.
Arnold, Margaret. *The Magdalene in the Reformation.* Cambridge: Harvard University Press, 2018.
Ashley, Benedict M. *The Dominicans.* 1990. Reprint, Eugene, OR: Wipf & Stock, 2009.
Atwood, Craig D. *Always Reforming: A History of Christianity Since 1300.* Macon, GA: Mercer University Press, 2001.
Audin, Jean. *History of the Life, Writings, and Doctrines of Luther.* Vol. 2. London: Dolman, 1854.
Avila, Teresa. *St. Teresa of Avila "The Way of Perfection": Study Edition.* Translated by Kieran Kavanaugh. Washington, DC: Institute of Carmelite Studies, 2013.
Avis, Paul. *The Church in the Theology of the Reformers.* 1981. Reprint, Eugene, OR: Wipf & Stock, 2002.
———. *Reconciling Theology: Conflict and Convergence in Theology and Church.* London: SCM, 2022.
Awes Freeman, Jennifer. "'And Who Is My Neighbor?' Historical Images of Christian Reponses to Pandemic." In *Threshold Dwellers in the Age of Global Pandemic*, edited by Eleazar S. Fernandez, 64-98. Eugene, OR: Pickwick Publications, 2022.

Bibliography

Badini Confalonieri, Luca. *Democracy in the Christian Church: An Historical, Theological and Political Case.* London: Bloomsbury, 2012.
Bahrych, Sharon. *Practical Disciplines of a Christian Life.* Bingley: Emerald House, 2016.
Bainton, Roland H. *Women of the Reformation in Germany and Italy.* Boston: Beacon, 1974.
Baker, Wayne. "Zwingli, Huldrych (1484–1531)." In *Encyclopedia of Protestantism*, edited by Hans. J. Hillerbrand, 4:892–903. New York: Routledge, 2004.
Barnes, Robin B. "Eschatology, Apocalypticism, and the Antichrist." In *T. & T. Clark Companion to Reformation Theology*, edited by David M. Whitford, 233–55. London: Bloomsbury, 2014.
Barnett, Christopher B. *Kierkegaard, Pietism and Holiness.* Burlington, VT: Ashgate, 2011.
Baronov, David. *Conceptual Foundations of Social Research Methods.* Milton Park: Taylor & Francis, 2015.
Barth, J. Robert. *Romanticism and Transcendence: Wordsworth, Coleridge, and the Religious Imagination.* Columbia: University of Missouri Press, 2003.
Barth, Karl. *The Knowledge of God and the Service of God according to the Teaching of the Reformation: Recalling the Scottish Confession of 1560.* Translated by J. L. M. Haire and Ian Henderson. 1938. Reprint, Eugene, OR: Wipf & Stock, 2005.
———. *The Theology of the Reformed Confessions, 1923.* Translated and annotated by Darrell L. Guder and Judith J. Guder. Columbia Series in Reformed Theology. Louisville: Westminster John Knox, 2005.
Bayer, Oswald. *Living by Faith: Justification and Sanctification.* Translated by Geoffrey W. Bromiley. Lutheran Quarterly Books. Grand Rapids: Eerdmans, 2003.
Baylor, Michael G. *The Radical Reformation.* Cambridge: Cambridge University Press, 1991.
Beeke, Jonathon D. *Duplex Regnum Christi: Christ's Twofold Kingdom in Reformed Theology.* Studies in Reformed Theology 40. Leiden: Brill, 2020.
Beeke, Joel R. *Revelation.* The Lectio Continua Expository Commentary on the New Testament. Grand Rapids: Reformation Heritage, 2016.
Bejczy, István P. *Erasmus and the Middle Ages: The Historical Consciousness of a Christian Humanist.* Brill's Studies in Intellectual History 106. Leiden: Brill, 2001.
Belt, Henk van den. *The Authority of Scripture in Reformed Theology: Truth and Trust.* Studies in Reformed Theology 17. Leiden: Brill, 2008.
Bender, Kimlyn J. *Reflections on Reformational Theology: Studies in the Theology of the Reformation, Karl Barth, and the Evangelical Tradition.* London: T. & T. Clark, 2021.
Berglar, Peter. *Thomas More: A Lonely Voice against the Power of the State.* New York: Scepter, 2009.
Berkouwer, Gerrit C. *Divine Election.* Grand Rapids: Eerdmans, 1960.
Bèze, Theodore de. *The Psalmes of David.* London: Yardley, 1590.
Biagioni, Mario. *The Radical Reformation and the Making of Modern Europe: A Lasting Heritage.* Studies in Medieval and Reformation Traditions 207. Leiden: Brill, 2016.
Billings, J. Todd. *Calvin, Participation, and the Gift: The Activity of Believers in Union with Christ.* Oxford: Oxford University Press, 2007.
Blacketer, Raymond A. "The Man in the Black Hat: Theodore Beza and the Reorientation of Early Reformed Historiography." In *Church and School in Early Modern Protestantism: Studies in Honor of Richard A. Muller on the Maturation of a Theological Tradition*, edited by Jordan Ballor et al., 227–42. Studies in the History of Christian Traditions 170. Leiden: Brill, 2013.

Bibliography

Bouley, Bradford A. *Pious Postmortems: Anatomy, Sanctity, and the Catholic Church in Early Modern Europe*. Philadelphia: University of Pennsylvania Press, 2017.

Bouwsma, William J. "Anxiety and the Formation of Early Modern Europe." In *After the Reformation: Essays in Honor of J. H. Hexter*, edited by Barbara C. Malament, 215–46. Philadelphia: University of Pennsylvania Press, 1980.

Bradstock, Andrew. *Faith in the Revolution: The Political Theologies of Müntzer and Winstanley*. London: SPCK, 1997.

Brady, Thomas A. "Social History." In *Reformation Europe: A Guide to Research*, edited by Steven E. Ozment, 161–81. Saint Louis: Center for Reformation Research, 1982.

Bray, John S. *Theodore Beza's Doctrine of Predestination*. Redwood City: Stanford University Press, 1971.

Brenz, Johannes. *Etlich Tractetli*. Augsburg: Philipp Ulhart, 1528.

Brondos, David A. *Redeeming the Gospel: The Christian Faith Reconsidered*. Minneapolis: Fortress, 2011.

Brown, David M. *Transformational Preaching: Theory and Practice*. College Station: Virtualbookworm.com, 2003.

Bubenheimer, Ulrich. *Wittenberg 1517–1522: Diskussions-, Aktionsgemeinschaft und Stadtreformation*. Spätmittelalter, Humanismus, Reformation 134. Tübingen: Mohr Siebeck, 2023.

Buckwalter Horst, Irvin. "Menno Simons: The Road to a Voluntary Church." In *The Dutch Dissenters: A Critical Companion to Their History and Ideas, with a Bibliographical Survey of Recent Research Pertaining to the Early Reformation in the Netherlands*, edited by Irvin Buckwalter Horst, 194–206. Kerkhistorische Bijdragen 13. Leiden: Brill, 1986.

Bullinger, Heinrich. *The Decades of Henry Bullinger, Minister of the Church of Zurich: The Fifth Decade*. Edited by Thomas Hardy. Parker Society. 1852. Reprint, Eugene, OR: Wipf & Stock, 2010.

Byrd, Charles Hannon, II. *Pentecostal Aspects of Early Sixteenth-Century Anabaptism*. Eugene, OR: Wipf & Stock, 2019.

Calvin, Jean. *Institutes of the Christian Religion*. Translated by Henry Beveridge. Peabody, MA: Hendrickson, 2008.

Cameron, Euan. *The European Reformation*. Oxford: Oxford University Press, 2012.

Campi, Emidio. "Was the Reformation a German Event?" In *The Myth of the Reformation*, edited by Peter Opitz, 9–31. Refo500 Academic Studies 4. Göttingen: Vandenhoeck & Ruprecht, 2013.

Campos, Heber C. de. *Doctrine in Development: Johannes Piscator and Debates over Christ's Active Obedience*. Grand Rapids: Reformation Heritage, 2017.

Cary, Phillip. *The Meaning of Protestant Theology: Luther, Augustine, and the Gospel That Gives Us Christ*. Grand Rapids: Baker Academic, 2019.

Castaldo, Chris. *Justified in Christ: The Doctrines of Peter Martyr Vermigli and John Henry Newman and Their Ecumenical Implications*. Eugene, OR: Pickwick Publications, 2017.

Chan, Suk Yu. *Heavenly Providence: A Historical Exploration of the Development of Calvin's Biblical Doctrine of Divine Providence*. Reformed Historical Theology 75. Göttingen: Vandenhoeck & Ruprecht, 2022.

Chemnitz, Martin. *The Two Natures in Christ*. St. Louis: Concordia, 1971.

Chibi, Andrew A. *Fear God, Honor the King: Magisterial Power and the Church in the Reformation, circa 1470–1600*. Eugene, OR: Pickwick Publications, 2020.

Bibliography

Christman, Robert J. *Doctrinal Controversy and Lay Religiosity in Late Reformation Germany: The Case of Mansfeld.* Studies in Medieval and Reformation Traditions 157. Leiden: Brill, 2011.

Christ-von Wedel, Christine. *Erasmus of Rotterdam: Advocate of a New Christianity.* Toronto: University of Toronto Press, 2013.

Clark, Stuart. *Vanities of the Eye: Vision in Early Modern European Culture.* Oxford: Oxford University Press, 2009.

Clooney, Francis X. *Theology After Vedanta: An Experiment in Comparative Theology.* Albany: State University of New York Press, 1993.

Collinson, Patrick. *From Cranmer to Sancroft: Essays on English Religion in the Sixteenth and Seventeenth Centuries.* London: Bloomsbury Academic, 2007.

———. *The Reformation.* London: Phoenix, 2013.

Conwell, Joseph F. *Impelling Spirit: Revisiting a Founding Experience, 1539, Ignatius of Loyola and His Companions: An Exploration into the Spirit and Aims of the Society of Jesus as Revealed in the Founders' Proposed Papal Letter Approving the Society.* Chicago: Loyola, 1997.

Corda, Salvatore. *Veritas Sacramenti: A Study in Vermigli's Doctrine of the Lord's Supper.* Zürcher Beiträge zur Reformationsgeschichte 6. Zürich: Theologischer, 1975.

Courey, David J. *What Has Wittenberg to Do with Azusa? Luther's Theology of the Cross and Pentecostal Triumphalism.* T&T Clark Theology. London: T. & T. Clark, 2015.

Courvoisier, Jaques. *Zwingli: A Reformed Theologian.* 1963. Reprint, Eugene, OR: Wipf & Stock, 2016.

Cranmer, Thomas. *The Works of Thomas Cranmer* . . . Edited by John Edmund Cox. Oxford: Oxford University Press, 1846.

Cross, Richard. *Communicatio Idiomatum: Reformation Christological Debates.* Oxford: Oxford University Press, 2019.

Cunliffe-Jones, Hubert, ed. *A History of Christian Doctrine.* 1978. Reprint, Scholars' Editions in Theology. London: Bloomsbury, 2006.

Curto, Diogo R. *Imperial Culture and Colonial Projects: The Portuguese-Speaking World from the Fifteenth to the Eighteenth Centuries.* New York: Berghahn, 2020.

Curtright, Travis. *Thomas More: Why Patron of Statesmen?* Lanham, MD: Lexington, 2015.

Dalferth, Ingolf U. *Crucified and Resurrected: Restructuring the Grammar of Christology.* Grand Rapids: Baker Academic, 2015.

Dealy, Ross. *The Stoic Origins of Erasmus' Philosophy of Christ.* Erasmus Studies. Toronto: University of Toronto Press, 2017.

DeJonge, Michael P. *Bonhoeffer on Resistance: The Word against the Wheel.* Oxford: Oxford University Press, 2018.

Delcorno, Pietro. *In the Mirror of the Prodigal Son: The Pastoral Uses of a Biblical Narrative (c. 1200–1550).* Commentaria 9. Leiden: Brill, 2017.

Delisle, Jean, and Judith Woodsworth. *Translators through History.* Rev. ed. Amsterdam: Benjamins, 2012.

Derksen, John D. *From Radicals to Survivors: Strasbourg's Religious Nonconformists over Two Generations, 1525–1570.* Bibliotheca Humanistica & Reformatorica 61. Leiden: Brill, 2021.

Di Renzo, Anthony. *American Gargoyles: Flannery O'Connor and the Medieval Grotesque.* Carbondale: Southern Illinois University Press, 1995.

Bibliography

Diaz, Elisheva I. *Wrestling for My Jewish Identity: An Eclipse with Reality.* Victoria: Friesen, 2017.

Dixon, C. Scott. *Protestants: A History from Wittenberg to Pennsylvania 1517–1740.* Malden, MA: Wiley-Blackwell, 2010.

Dominiak, Paul A. *Richard Hooker: The Architecture of Participation.* T & T Clark Studies in English Theology. London: T. & T. Clark, 2019.

Donnelly, John P. *Calvinism and Scholasticism in Vermigli's Doctrine of Man and Grace.* Studies in Medieval and Reformation Traditions 18. Leiden: Brill, 1976.

———. *Jesuit Writings of the Early Modern Period: 1540–1640.* Indianapolis: Hackett, 2006.

Dorner, Isaak A. *History of Protestant Theology.* Vol. 1. Edinburgh: T. & T. Clark, 1871.

Dost, Timothy P. *Renaissance Humanism in Support of the Gospel in Luther's Early Correspondence: Taking All Things Captive.* 2001. Reprint, Oxford: Routledge, 2017.

Dowey, Edward. "Heinrich Bullinger as Theologian: Thematic, Comprehensive, and Schematic." In *Architect of Reformation: An Introduction to Heinrich Bullinger, 1504–1575*, edited by Bruce Gordon and Emidio Campi, 35–66. 2004. Reprint, Eugene, OR: Wipf & Stock, 2019.

Drake, K. J. *The Flesh of the Word: The Extra Calvinisticum from Zwingli to Early Orthodoxy.* Oxford: Oxford University Press, 2021.

Duffy, Eamon. *Reformation Divided: Catholics, Protestants and the Conversion of England.* London: Bloomsbury Academic, 2017.

Dupré, Louis. "Unio Mystica: The State and the Experience." In *Mystical Union in Judaism, Christianity, and Islam: An Ecumenical Dialogue*, edited by Moshe Idel and Bernard McGinn, 3–26. 1989. Reprint, London: Bloomsbury, 2016.

Durant, Will. *The Complete Story of Civilization.* Vol. 1. New York: Simon & Schuster, 2014.

Dyck, Cornelius J., ed. *An Introduction to Mennonite History: A Popular History of the Anabaptists and the Mennonites.* Scottdale, PA: Herald, 1993.

Egan, Harvey D. *Ignatius Loyola the Mystic.* The Way of the Christian Mystics 5. 1987. Reprint, Eugene, OR: Wipf & Stock, 2020.

Ehmer, Hermann. "Johannes Brenz (1499–1570)." In *The Reformation Theologians: An Introduction to Theology in the Early Modern Period*, edited by Carter Lindberg, 124–40. Great Theologians. Oxford: Blackwell, 2002.

Eire, Carlos M. N. *Reformations: The Early Modern World, 1450–1650.* New Haven: Yale University Press, 2016.

———. *War against the Idols: The Reformation of Worship from Erasmus to Calvin.* Cambridge: Cambridge University Press, 1986.

Eppley, David. "Richard Hooker on the Un-Conditionality of Predestination." In *Richard Hooker and the English Reformation*, edited by W. J. Torrance Kirby, 63–78. Studies in Early Modern Religious Reforms 2. Dordrecht: Kluwer Academic, 2013.

Erasmus, Desiderius. *The Christian's Manual.* London: A. J. Valpy, 1816.

Essary, Kirk. *Erasmus and Calvin on the Foolishness of God: Reason and Emotion in the Christian Philosophy.* Erasmus Studies. Toronto: University of Toronto Press, 2017.

Estep, William R. *The Anabaptist Story: An Introduction to Sixteenth-Century Anabaptism.* Grand Rapids: Eerdmans, 1996.

Evener, Vincent. "Andreas Bodenstein von Karlstadt." In *Protestants and Mysticism in Reformation Europe*, edited by Ronald K. Rittgers and Vincent Evener, 78–99. St. Andrews Studies in Reformation History. Leiden: Brill, 2019.

Bibliography

———. *Enemies of the Cross: Suffering, Truth, and Mysticism in the Early Reformation.* Oxford: Oxford University Press, 2021.

Fairbairn, Donald, and Ryan M. Reeves. *The Story of Creeds and Confessions: Tracing the Development of the Christian Faith.* Grand Rapids: Baker Academic, 2019.

Farmer, Craig S. *The Gospel of John in the Sixteenth Century: The Johannine Exegesis of Wolfgang Musculus.* Oxford: Oxford University Press, 1997.

Fesko, John V. *Beyond Calvin: Union with Christ and Justification in Early Modern Reformed Theology (1517–1700).* Reformed Historical Theology 20. Göttingen: Vandenhoeck & Ruprecht, 2012.

———. *What Is Justification by Faith Alone?* Basics of the Reformed Faith. Phillipsburg: P & R Publishing, 2008.

Finnis, John. *Natural Law and Natural Rights.* Oxford: Oxford University Press, 2011.

Fitzgerald, Robert. *The Soul of Sponsorship: The Friendship of Fr. Ed Dowling, S.J. and Bill Wilson in Letters.* Center City: Hazelden, 2011.

Flacius Illyricus, Matthias. *Von Der Gerechtigkeit Wider Osiandrum.* Magdeburg: Christian Rödinger, 1552.

Forde, Gerald O. *Justification by Faith: A Matter of Death and Life.* 1982. Reprint, Eugene, OR: Wipf & Stock, 2012.

Franks, Robert. *A History of the Doctrine of the Work of Christ.* 1918. Reprint, Eugene, OR: Wipf & Stock, 2001.

Friesen, Abraham. "Erasmus." In *T. & T. Clark Handbook of Anabaptism*, edited by Brian C. Brewer, 457–76. London: T. & T. Clark, 2021.

———. *Menno Simons: Dutch Reformer Between Luther, Erasmus, and the Holy Spirit a Study in the Problem Areas of Menno Scholarship.* Bloomington: Xlibris, 2015.

Friesen, Leonard G. *Mennonites in the Russian Empire and the Soviet Union: Through Much Tribulation.* Tsarist and Soviet Mennonite Studies. Toronto: University of Toronto Press, 2022.

Furcha, Edward J. *Schwenckfeld's Concept of the New Man: A Study in the Anthropology of Caspar Von Schwenckfeld as Set Forth in His Major Theological Writings.* Pennsburg: Board of Publication of the Schwenkfelder Church, 1970.

Furnal, Joshua. *Catholic Theology After Kierkegaard.* Oxford: Oxford University Press, 2016.

Gadamer, Hans G. *Hans-Georg Gadamer on Education, Poetry, and History: Applied Hermeneutics.* SUNY Series in Contemporary Continental Philosophy. Albany: State University of New York Press, 2016.

Gamman, Andrew. *Church Invisible: Insights for Today's Church from the Sixteenth Century Radicals.* Whangaparaoa, NZ: Kereru, 2013.

Gardiner Rodgers, Katherine. "The Lessons of Ghethsemane: De Tristitia Christi." In *The Cambridge Companion to Thomas More*, edited by George M. Logan, 239–64. Cambridge Companions to Religion Cambridge: Cambridge University Press, 2011.

Garrett, Duane A. *The Problem of the Old Testament: Hermeneutical, Schematic, and Theological Approaches.* Downers Grove, IL: InterVarsity, 2020.

Gasquet, Francis A. *The Eve of the Reformation: Studies in the Religious Life and Thought of the English People in the Period Preceding the Rejection of the Roman Jurisdiction by Henry VIII.* 1900. Reprint, Gravesend: Bell, 2020.

Gelpi, Donald L. *The Gracing of Human Experience: Rethinking the Relationship between Nature and Grace.* 2007. Reprint, Eugene, OR: Wipf & Stock, 2008.

Bibliography

George, Timothy. *Galatians: The Christian Standard Commentary*. Brentwood, TN: Broadman & Holman, 2020.

———. *Reading Scripture with the Reformers*. Downers Grove, IL: InterVarsity, 2011.

———. *Theology of the Reformers*. Brentwood, TN: Broadman & Holman, 2013.

Gerrish, Brian A. *Continuing the Reformation: Essays on Modern Religious Thought*. Chicago: University of Chicago Press, 1993.

———. *The Old Protestantism and the New: Essays on the Reformation Heritage*. 1982. London: Bloomsbury, 2004.

Gogan, Brian. *The Common Corps of Christendom: Ecclesiological Themes in the Writings of Sir Thomas More*. Studies in the History of Christian Thought 26. Leiden: Brill, 2022.

Gordon, Bruce. *Zwingli: God's Armed Prophet*. New Haven: Yale University Press, 2021.

Gordon, Bruce. "The Changing Face of Protestant History and Identity in the Sixteenth Century." In *Protestant History and Identity in Sixteenth-Century Europe*, edited by Bruce Gordon, 2:1–22. St. Andrews Studies in Reformation History. Brookfield, VT: Ashgate, 1996.

Goudriaan, Aza. "Reformed Theology and the Church Fathers." In *The Oxford Handbook of Reformed Theology*, edited by Michael Allen and Scott R. Swain, 9–23. Oxford: Oxford University Press, 2020.

Graybill, Gregory. *Evangelical Free Will: Phillipp Melanchthon's Doctrinal Journey on the Origins of Faith*. Oxford: Oxford University Press, 2010.

Gregory, Brad S. *The Unintended Reformation: How a Religious Revolution Secularized Society*. Cambridge, MA: Belnap, 2015.

Grendler, Paul F. *The Universities of the Italian Renaissance*. Baltimore: Johns Hopkins University Press, 2004.

Grenz, Stanley J. *The Social God and the Relational Self: A Trinitarian Theology of the Imago Dei*. Louisville: Westminster John Knox, 2001.

Gritsch, Eric W. *Thomas Müntzer: A Tragedy of Errors*. Minneapolis: Fortress, 2006.

Grumbach, A. von. *Schriften*. Edited by Peter Matheson. Gütersloh: Gütersloher, 2010.

Gustafson, Hans-Fredrik. *The Genesis of Cajetan's Exegesis: Motivation and Initial Quest*. Madison: University of Wisconsin–Madison, 1993.

Haberkern, Phillip N. *Patron Saint and Prophet: Jan Hus in the Bohemian and German Reformations*. Oxford: Oxford University Press, 2016.

Habsburg, Maximilian von. *Catholic and Protestant Translations of the Imitatio Christi, 1425–1650: From Late Medieval Classic to Early Modern Bestseller*. St. Andrews Studies in Reformation History. Aldershot, UK: Ashgate, 2011.

Hafemann, Scott J. *Paul: Servant of the New Covenant: Pauline Polarities in Eschatological Perspective*. Tübingen: Mohr Siebeck, 2020.

Haga, Joar. *Was There a Lutheran Metaphysics?: The Interpretation of Communicatio Idiomatum in Early Modern Lutheranism*. Refo500 Academic Studies 2. Göttingen: Vandenhoeck & Ruprecht, 2012.

Hagen, Kenneth. *Hebrews Commenting from Erasmus to Beze*. Beiträge zur Geschichte der biblischen Exegese 23. 1981. Reprint, Eugene, OR: Wipf & Stock, 2011.

Hahn, Scott. *Scripture Matters: Essays on Reading the Bible from the Heart of the Church*. Steubenville, OH: Emmaus Road, 2003.

Hall, H. Ashley. *Philip Melanchthon and the Cappadocians: A Reception of Greek Patristic Sources in the Sixteenth Century*. Göttingen: Vandenhoeck & Ruprecht, 2014.

BIBLIOGRAPHY

Hall, Sam. *Shakespeare's Folly: Philosophy, Humanism, Critical Theory*. New York: Routledge, 2016.

Hamm, Berndt. *The Early Luther: Stages in a Reformation Reorientation*. Grand Rapids: Eerdmans, 2014.

Hannula, Richard M. *Heralds of the Reformation: Thirty Biographies of Sheer Grace*. Moscow, ID: Canon, 2016.

Harrison, Peter. *The Bible, Protestantism, and the Rise of Natural Science*. Cambridge: Cambridge University Press, 2001.

Helm, Paul. *John Calvin's Ideas*. Oxford: Oxford University Press, 2004.

Hendrix, Scott H. "Rerooting the Faith: The Coherence and Significance of the Reformation." *The Princeton Seminary Bulletin* 21 (2000) 63–80.

———. "The Use of Scripture in Establishing Protestantism. The Case of Urbanus Rhegius." In *The Bible in the Sixteenth Century*, edited by David Steinmetz, 37–49. Durham: Duke University Press, 1990.

Herrmann, Erik. "On the Babylonian Captivity of the Church (1520)." In *How the Reformation Began: The Quincentennial Perspective*, edited by Anna M. Johnson and Nicholas Hopman, 62–71. Eugene, OR: Pickwick Publications, 2022.

Hicks, Zac. *Worship by Faith Alone: Thomas Cranmer, the Book of Common Prayer, and the Reformation of Liturgy*. Dynamics of Christian Worship. Downers Grove, IL: InterVarsity, 2023.

Hildebrand, Pierrick. "Heinrich Bullinger (1504–1575) and the Covenant of Works." In *Covenant: A Vital Element of Reformed Theology: Biblical, Historical and Systematic-Theological Perspectives*, edited by Hans Burger et al., 254–66. Studies in Reformed Theology. Leiden: Brill, 2021.

Hinlicky, Paul R. *Beloved Community: Critical Dogmatics after Christendom*. Grand Rapids: Eerdmans, 2015.

Hollenback, Jess B. *Mysticism: Experience, Response, and Empowerment*. University Park: Pennsylvania State University Press, 1996.

Hoogstraten, Barth. *The Debaters*. Morrisville, NC: Lulu, 2015.

Hooker, Richard. "Of the Laws of Ecclesiastical Polity, Book 1." In *Richard Hooker, of the Laws of Ecclesiastical Polity: A Critical Edition with Modern Spelling*, edited by Arthur S. McGrade. Oxford: Oxford University Press, 2013.

———. *The Works of Mr. Richard Hooker: In Eight Books,* Volume 3: *Of the Laws of Ecclesiastical Polity, with Several Other Treatises and a General Index: Also, a Life of the Author*. London: Clarke, 1821.

Hopper, David H. *Divine Transcendence and the Culture of Change*. Grand Rapids: Eerdmans, 2010.

Hughes, Philip E. *Lefèvre: Pioneer of Ecclesiastical Renewal in France*. Grand Rapids: Eerdmans, 1984.

Hughes, Thomas. *Loyola and the Educational System of the Jesuits*. London: Heinemann, 1892.

Hussey, Ian. *The Soteriological Use of Call by Paul and Luke*. Eugene, OR: Wipf & Stock, 2018.

Ignatius of Loyola. *Ignatius of Loyola: The Spiritual Exercises and Selected Works*. Chicago: Loyola University Press, 1991.

———. *Letters of St. Ignatius of Loyola*. Selected and translated by William J. Young. Chicago: Loyola University Press, 1959.

———. *The Spiritual Exercises of St. Ignatius of Loyola*. n. p.: FV Éditions, 2016.

Bibliography

Iserloh, Erwin. "The Development of Denominations in the Sixteenth and Seventeenth Centuries." In *History of the Church: Reformation and Counter Reformation*, edited by Hubert Jedin and John Dolan, 5:419–30. London: Burns & Oates, 1980.

Istafanous, Abd-el-Masih. *Calvin's Doctrine of Biblical Authority*. Eugene, OR: Wipf & Stock, 2010.

Ives, Eric W. *The Reformation Experience: Living Through the Turbulent 16th Century*. Oxford: Lion, 2012.

Jackson, Gregory L. *Catholic, Lutheran, Protestant: A Doctrinal Comparison of Three Christian Confessions*. Morrisville, NC: Lulu, 2010.

Jacobs, Alan. *The Book of Common Prayer: A Biography*. Princeton: Princeton University Press, 2019.

James, David. *Hegel's Philosophy of Right: Subjectivity and Ethical Life*. London: Bloomsbury Academic, 2007.

James, Frank A, III. "Introduction. *Nunc Peregrinus Oberrat*: Peter Martyr in Context." In *Peter Martyr Vermigli and the European Reformations: Semper Reformanda*, edited by Frank A. James III, xiii–xxv. Studies in the History of Christian Traditions 115. Leiden: Brill, 2021.

———. "Theologies of Salvation in the Reformation and Counter-Reformation: An Introduction." In *Christian Theologies of Salvation: A Comparative Introduction*, edited by Justin S. Holcomb, 181–90. New York: New York University Press, 2017.

Janse, Wim. *Albert Hardenberg als Theologe: Profil eines Bucer-Schülers*. Studies in the History of Christian Thought 57. Leiden: Brill, 2021.

Janz, Dennis. *Luther and Late Medieval Thomism: A Study in Theological Anthropology*. Waterloo, ON: Wilfrid Laurier University Press, 1983.

Johnston, Wade. *The Devil behind the Surplice: Matthias Flacius and John Hooper on Adiaphora*. Eugene, OR: Pickwick Publications, 2018.

Jones, Rufus M. *Spiritual Reformers in the 16th and 17th Centuries*. 1914. Reprint, Eugene, OR: Wipf & Stock, 2005.

Jongeneel, Jan A. B. *Jesus Christ in World History: His Presence and Representation in Cyclical and Linear Settings*. Studies in the Intercultural History of Christianity 149. Frankfurt: Lang, 2009.

Joyce, A. J. *Richard Hooker and Anglican Moral Theology*. Oxford: Oxford University Press, 2012.

Kaiser, Christopher B. *The Doctrine of God: A Historical Survey*. Rev. ed. Eugene, OR: Wipf & Stock, 2001.

Kame, Greg. *Predestination: An Introduction to Reformed Soteriology*. Eugene, OR: Resource Publications, 2021.

Kärkkäinen, Veli-Matti. *An Introduction to Ecclesiology: Historical, Global, and Interreligious Perspectives*. Downers Grove, IL: InterVarsity, 2021.

———. *Hope and Community*. Vol. 5: *A Constructive Christian Theology for the Pluralistic World*. Grand Rapids: Eerdmans, 2017.

Karlberg, Mark W. *Covenant Theology in the Reformed Perspective: Collected Essays and Book Reviews in Historical, Biblical, and Systematic Theology*. Eugene, OR: Wipf & Stock, 2000.

Karlstadt, Andreas B., von. "On the Priesthood and Sacrifice of Christ." In *The Eucharistic Pamphlets of Andreas Bodenstein von Karlstadt*, edited by Amy Nelson Burnett, 89–109. Early Modern Studies. University Park: Penn State University Press, 2011.

Kaufmann, Thomas. *A Short Life of Martin Luther*. Grand Rapids: Eerdmans, 2016.

Bibliography

Kayamba, Lawum. *The Social and Political Dimension of the Kingdom of God in Mark.* Bloomington: WestBow, 2021.

Kee, Howard C. *Christianity: A Social and Cultural History.* London: Macmillan, 1991.

Kelley, Donald R. *The Beginning of Ideology: Consciousness and Society in the French Reformation.* Cambridge: Cambridge University Press, 1981.

Kiefer, Frederick. *Writing on the Renaissance Stage: Written Words, Printed Pages, Metaphoric Books.* Newark: University of Delaware Press, 1996.

Kiefer Lewalski, Barbara. *Donne's Anniversaries and the Poetry of Praise: The Creation of a Symbolic Mode.* Princeton: Princeton University Press, 2015.

Kilcrease, Jack D. *The Self-Donation of God: A Contemporary Lutheran Approach to Christ and His Benefits.* Eugene, OR: Wipf & Stock, 2013.

Kim, Yosep. *The Identity and the Life of the Church: John Calvin's Ecclesiology in the Perspective of His Anthropology.* Eugene, OR: Pickwick Publications, 2014.

Kirby, Torrance. *Persuasion and Conversion: Essays on Religion, Politics, and the Public Sphere in Early Modern England.* Studies in the History of Christian Traditions 166. Leiden: Brill, 2013.

———. *Richard Hooker, Reformer and Platonist.* Aldershot, UK: Ashgate, 2007.

Kloes, Andrew. *The German Awakening: Protestant Renewal after the Enlightenment, 1815–1848.* Oxford: Oxford University Press, 2019.

Kolb, Robert. "Human Nature, the Fall, and the Will." In *T. & T. Clark Companion to Reformation Theology*, edited by David M. Whitford, 14–31. T. & T. Clark Companions. London: T. & T. Clark, 2014.

———. "Human Performance and the Righteousness of Faith: Martin Chemnitz's Anti-Roman Polemic in Formula of Concord III." In *By Faith Alone. Esssays on Justification in Honor of Gerhard O. Forde*, edited by Joseph A. Burgess and Mark Kolden, 125–39. Grand Rapids: Eerdmans, 2004.

———. *Lutheran Ecclesiastical Culture, 1550–1675.* Brill's Companions to the Christian Tradition 11. Leiden: Brill, 2008.

———. *Martin Luther as He Lived and Breathed: Recollections of the Reformer.* Cascade Companions. Eugene, OR: Cascade Books, 2018.

Koons, Robert C. *A Lutheran's Case for Roman Catholicism: Finding a Lost Path Home.* Eugene, OR: Cascade Books, 2020.

Korbel, Joseph. *Detente in Europe: Real or Imaginary?* Princeton: Princeton University Press, 2015.

Kreeft, Peter. *Catholics and Protestants: What Can We Learn from Each Other?* San Francisco: Ignatius, 2017.

Kreitzer, Beth. *Reforming Mary: Changing Images of the Virgin Mary in Lutheran Sermons of the Sixteenth Century.* Oxford: Oxford University Press, 2004.

Krey, Philip D. W. "Lefèvre d'Etaples, Jacques (c. 1455–1536)." In *Historical Handbook of Major Biblical Interpreters*, edited by Donald K. McKim, 204–8. Downers Grove, IL: InterVarsity, 1998.

Kroeker, Greta G. *Erasmus in the Footsteps of Paul: A Pauline Theologian.* Toronto: University of Toronto Press, 2011.

Kurtz, Johann H. *Church History.* Vol. 2. New York: Funk & Wagnalls, 1894.

Kyle, Richard G. *God's Watchman: John Knox's Faith and Vocation.* Eugene, OR: Pickwick Publications, 2014.

LaBelle, Joseph T. *From Strength to Strength: Seven Timeless Virtues for Christian Discipleship.* Eugene, OR: Wipf & Stock, 2020.

Bibliography

Lai, Pan-Chiu. *Towards a Trinitarian Theology of Religions: A Study of Paul Tillich's Thought*. Kampen: Kok Pharos, 1994.

Lane, Anthony N. S. *Justification by Faith in Catholic-Protestant Dialogue*. London: Bloomsbury, 2006.

———. *The Regensburg Article 5 on Justification: Inconsistent Patchwork or Substance of True Doctrine?* Oxford: Oxford University Press, 2019.

Larsen, David L. *The Company of the Preachers*. Grand Rapids: Kregel, 1998.

Leith, John H. *John Calvin's Doctrine of the Christian Life*. 1989. Reprint, Eugene, OR: Wipf & Stock, 2010.

Leithart, Peter J. *The End of Protestantism: Pursuing Unity in a Fragmented Church*. Grand Rapids: Brazos, 2016.

Lenski, R. C. H. *Interpretation of St. Matthew's Gospel, Chapters 15-28*. Minneapolis: Augsburg Fortress, 1998.

Leo, Russ. *Tragedy as Philosophy in the Reformation World*. Oxford: Oxford University Press, 2019.

Leppin, Volker. "Luther's Mystical Roots." In *Martin Luther: A Christian between Reforms and Modernity (1517-2017)*, edited by Alberto Melloni, 157-72. Berlin: de Gruyter, 2017.

———. *Martin Luther: A Late Medieval Life*. Grand Rapids: Baker Academic, 2017.

Leuenberger, Samuel. *Archbishop Cranmer's Immortal Bequest: The Book of Common Prayer of the Church of England: An Evangelistic Liturgy*. 1990. Reprint, Eugene, OR: Wipf & Stock, 2004.

Lewis, Simon. *Anti-Methodism and Theological Controversy in Eighteenth-Century England: The Struggle for True Religion*. Oxford: Oxford University Press, 2022.

Lindberg, Carter. *The European Reformations*. 3rd ed. Hoboken, NJ: Wiley, 2021.

———. "Introduction." In *The Reformation Theologians: An Introduction to Theology in the Early Modern Period*, edited by Carter Lindberg, 1-16. Great Theologians. Malden, MA: Blackwell, 2002.

———, ed. *The Reformation Theologians: An Introduction to Theology in the Early Modern Period*. Great Theologians. Oxford: Wiley, 2017.

———. *The Third Reformation: Charismatic Movements and the Lutheran Tradition*. Macon, GA: Mercer University Press, 1983.

Littlejohn, W. Bradford. *Richard Hooker: A Companion to His Life and Work*. Cascade Companions. Eugene, OR: Cascade Books, 2015.

Locher, Gottfried W. *Zwingli's Thought: New Perspectives*. Studies in the History of Christian Thought 25. Leiden: Brill, 2022.

Locke, Kenneth A. *The Church in Anglican Theology: A Historical, Theological and Ecumenical Exploration*. 2009. Reprint, London: Routledge, 2016.

Lodyzhenskii, M. V. *Light Invisible: Satisfying the Thirst for Happiness*. Jordanville, NY: Holy Trinity Publications, 2011.

Loewen, Harry. *Ink against the Devil: Luther and His Opponents*. Waterloo, ON: Wilfrid Laurier University Press, 2015.

———. *Luther and the Radicals: Another Look at Some Aspects of the Struggle between Luther and the Radical Reformers*. Waterloo, ON: Wilfrid Laurier University Press, 2010.

Loewen, Jacob A., and Wesley J. Prieb. *Only the Sword of the Spirit*. Winnipeg, MB: Kindred Productions, 1997.

BIBLIOGRAPHY

Long, Roy. *Martin Luther and His Legacy: A Perspective on 500 Years of Reformation.* Morrisville, NC: Lulu, 2017.

Lugioyo, Brian. *Martin Bucer's Doctrine of Justification: Reformation Theology and Early Modern Irenicism.* Oxford: Oxford University Press, 2010.

Luther, Martin. *Martin Luther on the Bondage of the Will: Written in Answer to the Diatribe of Erasmus on Free-Will. First Pub. in the Year of Our Lord 1525.* London: Bensley, 1823.

Luther, Timothy C. *Hegel's Critique of Modernity: Reconciling Individual Freedom and the Community.* Lanham, MD: Lexington, 2009.

Mabry, Eddie L. *Balthasar Hubmaier's Understanding of Faith.* Lanham, MD: University Press of America, 1998.

Maier, Paul L. *Caspar Schwenckfeld on the Person and Work of Christ: A Study of Schwenckfeldian Theology at Its Core.* 1959. Reprint, Eugene, OR: Wipf & Stock, 2004.

Mallinson, Jeffrey. *Faith, Reason, and Revelation in Theodore Beza, 1519–1605.* Oxford: Oxford University Press, 2003.

Malloy, Christopher J. *Engrafted Into Christ: A Critique of the Joint Declaration.* American University Studies. Series VII, Theology and Religion 233. New York: Lang, 2005.

Manetsch, Scott M. "'I Have the Word of God': Scripture, Interpretation, and Crespin's History of the Martyrs." In *The Reformation and the Irrepressible Word of God: Interpretation, Theology, and Practice*, edited by Scott M. Manetsch, 15–39. Downers Grove, IL: InterVarsity, 2019.

Marius, Richard. *Thomas More: A Biography.* Cambridge, MA: Harvard University Press, 1999.

Marsden, George M. *The Soul of the American University: From Protestant Establishment to Established Nonbelief.* Oxford: Oxford University Press, 1994.

Marshall, Peter. *Beliefs and the Dead in Reformation England.* Oxford: Oxford University Press, 2002.

Martens, Gottfried. *Die Rechtfertigung des Sünders: Rettungshandeln Gottes oder Historisches Interpretament? : Grundentscheidungen Lutherischer Theologie und Kirche bei der Behandlung des Themas "Rechtfertigung" im Ökumenischen Kontext.* Forschungen zur systematischen und ökumenischen Theologie 64. Göttingen: Vandenhoeck & Ruprecht, 1992.

Martin, Craig. *Subverting Aristotle: Religion, History, and Philosophy in Early Modern Science.* Baltimore: Johns Hopkins University Press, 2014.

Maruyama, Tadataka. *Calvin's Ecclesiology: A Study in the History of Doctrine.* Grand Rapids: Eerdmans, 2022.

Matheson, Peter. "Argula von Grumbach." In *The Reformation Theologians. An Introduction to Theology in the Early Modern Period*, edited by Carter Lindberg, 94–108. Great Theologians. Oxford: Wiley, 2002.

———. *Argula von Grumbach (1492–1554/7): A Woman before Her Time.* Eugene, OR: Cascade Books, 2013.

Mathiasen Stopa, Sasja. *Soli Deo Honor et Gloria: Honour and Glory in the Theology of Martin Luther.* Munich: LIT, 2021.

Mauldin, Joshua. *Barth, Bonhoeffer, and Modern Politics.* Oxford: Oxford University Press, 2021.

Maxfield, John A. *Luther's Lectures on Genesis and the Formation of Evangelical Identity.* Kirksville, MO: Trueman State University Press, 2008.

Bibliography

McCormack, Bruce L. *Justification in Perspective: Historical Developments and Contemporary Challenges.* Grand Rapids: Baker Academic, 2006.

McCutcheon, Elizabeth. "More's Rhetoric." In *The Cambridge Companion to Thomas More*, edited by George M. Logan, 46–68. Cambridge Companions to Religion. Cambridge: Cambridge University Press, 2011.

McDonnell, Kilian. *John Calvin, the Church and the Eucharist.* Princeton: Princeton University Press, 1967.

McGlasson, Paul C. *Church Doctrine.* Vol. 3: *Creation.* Eugene, OR: Cascade Books, 2015.

McGrath, Alister E. *Christian Theology: An Introduction.* Oxford: Wiley, 2011.

———. *Historical Theology: An Introduction to the History of Christian Thought.* Oxford: Wiley, 2022.

———. *Iustitia Dei: A History of the Christian Doctrine of Justification.* Cambridge: Cambridge University Press, 2020.

———. *Reformation Thought: An Introduction.* Oxford: Wiley, 2012.

McKee, Elsie A. *Katharina Schütz Zell: The Writings, a Critical Edition.* Leiden: Brill, 1999.

———. *Katharina Schütz Zell.* Vol. 1: *The Life and Thought of a Sixteenth-Century Reformer.* Studies in Medieval and Reformation Thought 69. Leiden: Brill, 2022.

McManamon, John M. *The Text and Contexts of Ignatius Loyola's "Autobiography."* New York: Fordham University Press, 2013.

McNeill, John T. *The History and Character of Calvinism.* Oxford: Oxford University Press, 1967.

Mead, James K. *Biblical Theology: Issues, Methods, and Themes.* Louisville: Westminster John Knox, 2007.

Meijering, E. P. *Melanchthon and Patristic Thought: The Doctrines of Christ and Grace, and the Trinity and the Creation.* Studies in the History of Christian Thought 32. Leiden: Brill, 1983.

Melanchthon, Philip. *The Augsburg Confession: The Confession of Faith, Which Was Submitted to His Imperial Majesty Charles V at the Diet of Augsburg in the Year 1530.* N.d.: DigiCat, 2022.

Mentzer, Raymond A. "Calvin and France." In *The Calvin Handbook*, edited by Herman J. Selderhuis, 78–86. Grand Rapids: Eerdmans, 2009.

Metzger, Bruce M. *The Bible in Translation: Ancient and English Versions.* Grand Rapids: Baker Academic, 2001.

Meyers, Jeffrey J. *The Lord's Service: The Grace of Covenant Renewal Worship.* Moscow, ID: Canon, 2003.

Middleton, Erasmus. *Biographia Evangelica; or, An Historical Account of . . . the Most Eminent and Evangelical Authors or Preachers.* Vol. 2. London: Paternoster, 1810.

Miller, Charles. *Richard Hooker and the Vision of God: Exploring the Origins of "Anglicanism."* Cambridge: James Clarke, 2013.

Miller, Joshua C. *Hanging by a Promise: The Hidden God in the Theology of Oswald Bayer.* Eugene, OR: Pickwick Publications, 2015.

Milner, Benjamin C. *Calvin's Doctrine of the Church.* Studies in the History of Christian Thought 5. Leiden: Brill, 1970.

Mitchell, Nathan D. "Reforms, Protestant and Catholic." In *The Oxford History of Christian Worship*, edited by Geoffrey Wainwright and Karen B. Westerfield Tucker, 307–50. Oxford: Oxford University Press, 2006.

Moeller, Bernd. *Imperial Cities and the Reformation: Three Essays.* Minneapolis: Fortress Press, 1972.

Bibliography

Moots, Glenn A. *Politics Reformed: The Anglo-American Legacy of Covenant Theology.* Columbia: University of Missouri Press, 2010.

More, Thomas. *A Thomas More Source Book.* Edited by Gerard B. Wegemer and Stephen W. Smith. Washington, DC: Catholic University of America Press, 2004.

———. *Utopia.* Mineola, NY: Dover, 2010.

Moss, Christina, and Gary K. Waite. "Argula von Grumbach, Katharina Schütz Zell, and Anabaptist and Jorist Women." In *Protestants and Mysticism in Reformation Europe*, edited by Ronald K. Rittgers and Vincent Evener, 159–78. St. Andrews Studies in Reformation History. Leiden: Brill, 2019.

Moynahan, Brian. *The Faith: A History of Christianity.* New York: Doubleday, 2007.

Muller, Richard A. *Calvin and the Reformed Tradition: On the Work of Christ and the Order of Salvation.* Grand Rapids: Baker Academic, 2012.

———. *The Unaccommodated Calvin: Studies in the Foundation of a Theological Tradition.* Oxford: Oxford University Press, 2000.

Mullett, Michael. *Historical Dictionary of the Reformation and Counter-Reformation.* Lanham, MD: Scarecrow, 2010.

Münzer, Thomas. *Revelation and Revolution: Basic Writings of Thomas Müntzer.* Edited by Michael G. Baylor. Bethlehem, PA: Lehigh University Press, 1993.

Muray, Leslie A. *Liberal Protestantism and Science.* Westport, CT: Greenwood, 2007.

Murray, Andrew. *The Secret of Christ Our Life.* Fort Washington: CLC Publications, 2018.

Murray, Stephen B. *Reclaiming Divine Wrath: A History of a Christian Doctrine and Its Interpretation.* Bern: Lang, 2011.

Myers, William D. "Ignatius Loyola and Martin Luther." In *A Companion to Ignatius of Loyola: Life, Writings, Spirituality, Influence*, edited by Robert A. Maryks, 141–58. Leiden: Brill, 2014.

Naphy, William G., ed. *Documents on the Continental Reformation.* London: Macmillan, 1996.

Neelands, David. "Predestination." In *A Companion to Richard Hooker*, edited by Torrance Kirby, 185–220. Leiden: Brill, 2008.

Nelson Burnett, Amy. *Debating the Sacraments: Print and Authority in the Early Reformation.* Oxford: Oxford University Press, 2019.

———. *Karlstadt and the Origins of the Eucharistic Controversy: A Study in the Circulation of Ideas.* Oxford: Oxford University Press, 2011.

Nichols, Aidan. *The Panther and the Hind: A Theological History of Anglicanism.* Edinburgh: T. & T. Clark, 1993.

Noll, Mark A., and Carolyn Nystrom. *Is the Reformation Over? An Evangelical Assessment of Contemporary Roman Catholicism.* Grand Rapids: Baker Academic, 2008.

Null, Ashley. *Thomas Cranmer's Doctrine of Repentance: Renewing the Power to Love.* Oxford: Oxford University Press, 2001.

Nystrom, Carolyn. *John Calvin: Sovereign Hope.* Downers Grove, IL: InterVarsity, 2002.

Oberdorfer, Bernd. "Law and Gospel and Two Realms: Lutheran Distinctions Revisited." In *Global Perspectives on the Reformation: Interactions between Theology, Politics and Economics*, edited by Anne Burkhardt and Simone Sinn, 31–42. Leipzig: Evangelische Verlagsanstalt, 2017.

O'Connor, Michael. *Cajetan's Biblical Commentaries: Motive and Method.* Leiden: Brill, 2017.

Old, Hughes Oliphant. *The Reading and Preaching of the Scriptures in the Worship of the Christian Church*, Volume 4. Grand Rapids: Eerdmans, 2002.

Bibliography

Olson, Oliver K. "Matthias Flacius." In *The Reformation Theologians. An Introduction to Theology in the Early Modern Period*, edited by Carter Lindberg, 83–93. Oxford: Blackwell, 2002.

Olson, Roger E. *The Story of Christian Theology: Twenty Centuries of Tradition and Reform*. Downers Grove, IL: InterVarsity, 2009.

O'Malley, John W. *Saints or Devils Incarnate? Studies in Jesuit History*. Leiden: Brill, 2013.

———. *Trent and All That: Renaming Catholicism in the Early Modern Era*. Cambridge, MA: Harvard University Press, 2009.

O'Regan, Cyril. *Gnostic Apocalypse: Jacob Boehme's Haunted Narrative*. Albany: State University of New York Press, 2012.

Otto, Rudolf. *West-Östliche Mystik*. München: Beck, 1971.

Oyer, John S. *Lutheran Reformers against Anabaptists: Luther, Melanchthon and Menius and the Anabaptists of Central Germany*. The Hague: Martinus Nijhof, 1964.

Ozment, Steven, ed. *The Age of Reform, 1250–1550: An Intellectual and Religious History of Late Medieval and Reformation Europe*. New Haven, CT: Yale University Press, 2020.

———. *Religion and Culture in the Renaissance and Reformation*. Kirksville, MO: Sixteenth Century Journal Publishers, 1989.

Pak, G. Sujin. *The Judaizing Calvin: Sixteenth-Century Debates over the Messianic Psalms*. Oxford: Oxford University Press, 2010.

———. *The Reformation of Prophecy: Early Modern Interpretations of the Prophet & Old Testament Prophecy*. Oxford: Oxford University Press, 2018.

Pannenberg, Wolfhart. *Jesus God and Man*. London: SCM, 1968.

Parker, T. H. L. *Calvin's Doctrine of the Knowledge of God*. 1952. Reprint, Eugene, OR: Wipf & Stock, 2015.

———. *John Calvin: A Biography*. Louisville: Westminster John Knox, 2006.

Partee, Charles. *The Theology of John Calvin*. Louisville: Westminster John Knox, 2008.

Pauck, Wilhelm, ed. *Melanchthon and Bucer*. Philadelphia: Westminster, 1969.

Paul, Joanne. *Thomas More*. Cambridge: Polity, 2017.

Paulson, Steven D. *Lutheran Theology*. London: Bloomsbury, 2011.

Pereira, Jairzinho L. *Augustine of Hippo and Martin Luther on Original Sin and Justification of the Sinner*. Göttingen: Vandenhoeck & Ruprecht, 2013.

Pérez-Romero, Antonio. *Subversion and Liberation in the Writings of St. Teresa of Avila*. Amsterdam: Rodopi, 1996.

Pettegree, Andrew. *The Reformation*, Volume 1: *Critical Concepts in Historical Studies*. London: Routledge, 2004.

Pfister, Oscar. *Christianity and Fear: A Study in History and in the Psychology and Hygiene of Religion*. London: Routledge, 2020.

Pietropaolo, Domenico. *Semiotics of the Christian Imagination: Signs of the Fall and Redemption*. London: Bloomsbury, 2020.

Pitkin, Barbara. *Calvin, the Bible, and History*. Oxford: Oxford University Press, 2020.

———. "Redefining Repentance: Calvin and Melanchthon." In *"Calvinus Præceptor Ecclesiæ": Papers of the International Congress on Calvin Research, Princeton, August 20–24, 2002*, edited by Herman J. Selderhuis, 275–86. Geneva: Droz, 2004.

Platt, John. *Reformed Thought and Scholasticism: The Arguments for the Existence of God in Dutch Theology, 1575–1650*. Leiden: Brill, 2022.

Plummer, Marjorie E. *From Priest's Whore to Pastor's Wife: Clerical Marriage and the Process of Reform in the Early German Reformation*. London: Routledge, 2016.

Bibliography

Pollmann, Judith. "A Different Road to God: The Protestant Experience of Conversion in the Sixteenth Century." In *Conversion to Modernities*, edited by Peter van der Veer, 47–64. New York: Routledge, 2014.

Polzer, Charles W. *Rules and Precepts of the Jesuit Missions of Northwestern New Spain.* Tucson: University of Arizona Press, 2016.

Ptaszynski, Maciej, and Kazimierz Bem. *Searching for Compromise? Interreligious Dialogue, Agreements, and Toleration in 16th-18th Century Eastern Europe.* Leiden: Brill, 2022.

Puff, Helmut. *Sodomy in Reformation Germany and Switzerland, 1400-1600.* Chicago: University of Chicago Press, 2003.

Purves, Andrew. *Pastoral Theology in the Classical Tradition.* Louisville, KY: Westminster John Knox, 2001.

Quatrini, Francesco. *Adam Boreel (1602-1665): A Collegiant's Attempt to Reform Christianity.* Leiden: Brill, 2020.

Quere, Ralph W. *Melanchthon's Christum Cognoscere: Christ's Efficacious Presence in the Eucharistic Theology of Melanchthon.* Leiden: Brill, 1977.

Räisänen-Schröder, Päivi. "Appeal and Survival of Anabaptism in Early Modern Germany." In *Lived Religion and the Long Reformation in Northern Europe c. 1300-1700*, edited by Raisa M. Toivo and Sari Katajala-Peltomaa, 104–30. Leiden: Brill, 2016.

Randall, Catharine. *Earthly Treasures: Material Culture and Metaphysics in the Heptaméron and Evangelical Narrative.* West Lafayette: Purdue University Press, 2007.

Razzall, Lucy. *Boxes and Books in Early Modern England.* Cambridge: Cambridge University Press, 2021.

Reardon, Bernard M. G. *Religious Thought in the Reformation.* London: Routledge, 2014.

Redding, Graham. *Prayer and the Priesthood of Christ.* London: T. & T. Clark, 2005.

Reid, Jonathan A. *King's Sister—Queen of Dissent*, Volume 1: *Marguerite of Navarre (1492-1549) and Her Evangelical Network.* Leiden: Brill, 2009.

Reilly, John P. *Cajetan's Notion of Existence.* Berlin: De Gruyter, 2015.

Rempel, John D. *The Lord's Supper in Anabaptism: A Study in the Christology of Balthasar Hubmaier, Pilgram Marpeck, and Dirk Philips.* Scottdale, PA: Herald, 1993.

Reynolds, Philip L. *How Marriage Became One of the Sacraments.* Cambridge: Cambridge University Press, 2016.

Riggs, John W. *Baptism in the Reformed Tradition: A Historical and Practical Theology.* Louisville, KY: Westminster John Knox, 2002.

Rittgers, Ronald K. *The Reformation of Suffering: Pastoral Theology and Lay Piety in Late Medieval and Early Modern Germany.* Oxford: Oxford University Press, 2012.

Riva, Franco. *Analogia e Univocità in Tommaso de Vio "Gaetano."* Milano: Vita e pensiero, 1995.

Robinson, Timothy. "The Banquet of Love: The Song of Songs in Reformed Sacramental Piety, 1586-1729." In *A Companion to the Song of Songs in the History of Spirituality*, edited by Timothy Robinson, 327–57. Leiden: Brill, 2021.

Rohr, John von. *The Covenant of Grace in Puritan Thought.* 1986. Reprint, Eugene, OR: Wipf & Stock, 2010.

Roper, Lyndal. *Martin Luther: Renegade and Prophet.* New York: Random House, 2017.

Rosenthal, Alexander S. *Crown under Law: Richard Hooker, John Locke, and the Ascent of Modern Constitutionalism.* Lanham, MD: Lexington, 2008.

Rouwendal, Pieter L. *Predestination and Preaching in Genevan Theology from Calvin to Pictet.* Kampen: Summum, 2017.

BIBLIOGRAPHY

Royer, Katherine. *The English Execution Narrative, 1200–1700*. London: Routledge, 2015.
Ruben, Aarne. *The Story of Lutheran Sects: "In Christ We Speak."* Newcastle upon Tyne: Cambridge Scholars, 2020.
Rummel, Erika. *The Confessionalization of Humanism in Reformation Germany*. Oxford: Oxford University Press, 2000.
Ruokanen, Miikka. *Trinitarian Grace in Martin Luther's The Bondage of the Will*. Oxford: Oxford University Press, 2021.
Rupp, Gordon. *Patterns of Reformation*. London: Epworth, 1969.
Russell, Paul A. *Lay Theology in the Reformation: Popular Pamphleteers in Southwest Germany 1521–1525*. Cambridge: Cambridge University Press, 2002.
Saarinen, Risto. *Luther and the Gift*. Tübingen: Mohr Siebeck, 2017.
Sabatier-Plantier, Henri de. *Rôle de Jacques Lefèvre d'Etaples à l'origine de La Réformation Française*. Toulouse: A. Chauvin et fils, 1870.
Scaer, David P. *James, the Apostle of Faith: A Primary Christological Epistle for the Persecuted Church*. 1994. Reprint, Eugene, OR: Wipf & Stock, 2004.
Schilling, Heinz. "Luther, Loyola, Calvin Und Die Europäische Neuzeit." *Archiv für Reformationsgeschichte* 85 (1994) 5–31.
Schmidt, Andreas. *Remain in Me: Contemplative Life in the World*. New York: Scepter, 2011.
Schütz Zell, Katharine. *Church Mother: The Writings of a Protestant Reformer in Sixteenth-Century Germany*. Translated by Elsie McKee. The Other Voice in Early Modern Europe. Chicago: University of Chicago Press, 2007.
Schwarz, Hans. *Method and Context as Problems for Contemporary Theology: Doing Theology in an Alien World*. Lewiston, NY: Mellen, 1991.
Schwenckfeld, Caspar, and Fred A. Grater. "Commentary on the Augusburg Confession." In *Caspar Schwenckfeld's Commentary on the Augsburg Confession: A Translation and Critical Introduction*, 47–188. Waterloo, ON: Wilfrid Laurier University, 1980.
Scotti, Paschal. *Galileo Revisited: The Galileo Affair in Context*. San Francisco: Ignatius, 2017.
Screech, Michael A. *Laughter at the Foot of the Cross*. Chicago: University of Chicago Press, 1997.
Secor, Philip B. *Richard Hooker: Prophet of Anglicanism*. London: Burns & Oates, 1999.
Seeberg, Reinhold. *Text-Book of the History of Doctrines, 2 Volumes: In the Ancient Church, and Middle Ages, Early Modern Ages*. 1905. Reprint, Eugene, OR: Wipf & Stock, 1997.
Séguenny, André. "Caspar von Schwenckfeld." In *The Reformation Theologians: An Introduction to Theology in the Early Modern Period*, edited by C. Lindberg, 351–62. Oxford: Wiley, 2017.
———. *The Christology of Caspar Schwenckfeld: Spirit and Flesh in the Process of Life Transformation*. Texts and Studies in Religion 35. Lewiston, NY: Mellen, 1987.
Selderhuis, Herman J. *Psalms 73–150*. Downers Grove, IL: InterVarsity, 2018.
Sheldrake, Philip. "George Herbert and The Country Parson." In *A History of Pastoral Care*, edited by G. R. Evans, 294–312. London: Cassell, 2000.
Shuger, Debora K. *Sacred Rhetoric: The Christian Grand Style in the English Renaissance*. Princeton: Princeton University Press, 2014.
Sider, Ronald J. *Andreas Bodenstein von Karlstadt: The Development of His Thought, 1517–1525*. Studies in Medieval and Reformation Thought 11. Leiden: Brill, 1974.
Simons, M. *The Complete Works of Menno Simons*. Elkhart, IN: Funk, 1871.

Bibliography

Simuţ, Corneliu C. *The Doctrine of Salvation in the Sermons of Richard Hooker*. Berlin: de Gruyter, 2005.

———. *Richard Hooker and His Early Doctrine of Justification: A Study of His Discourse of Justification*. Aldershot, UK: Ashgate, 2005.

Sklar, Peggy A. *St. Ignatius of Loyola: In God's Service*. New York: Paulist, 2001.

Smith, Barry D. *The Meaning of Jesus' Death: Reviewing the New Testament's Interpretations*. London: Bloomsbury, 2016.

Snyder, C. Arnold. *Faith and Toleration: A Reformation Debate Revisited*. Winnipeg: Canadian Mennonite University Press, 2018.

Soulen, Richard N. *Sacred Scripture: A Short History of Interpretation*. Louisville: Westminster John Knox, 2009.

Spencer, Stephen. *SCM Studyguide to Anglicanism*. London: SCM, 2021.

Spijker, Willem van 't. *Calvin: A Brief Guide to His Life and Thought*. Louisville: Westminster John Knox, 2009.

———. *The Ecclesiastical Offices in the Thought of Martin Bucer*. Studies in Medieval and Reformation Thought 57. Leiden: Brill, 1996.

Spinks, Bryan D. *Do This in Remembrance of Me: The Eucharist from the Early Church to the Present Day*. London: SCM, 2014.

———. *Reformation and Modern Rituals and Theologies of Baptism: From Luther to Contemporary Practices*. Aldershot, UK: Ashgate, 2006.

Sproul, R. C. *Faith Alone: The Evangelical Doctrine of Justification*. Grand Rapids: Baker, 1999.

Stackhouse, John G. *Humble Apologetics: Defending the Faith Today*. Oxford: Oxford University Press, 2006.

Steinmetz, David. *Calvin in Context*. 2nd ed. Oxford: Oxford University Press, 2010.

Steinmetz, D.C. *Reformers in the Wings: From Geiler von Kaysersberg to Theodore Beza*. Oxford University Press, 2001.

Stephenson, Barry. *Performing the Reformation: Public Ritual in the City of Luther*. Oxford: Oxford University Press, 2010.

Stewart, Alison G. *Before Bruegel: Sebald Beham and the Origins of Peasant Festival Imagery*. London: Routledge, 2017.

Stewart, Quentin D. *Lutheran Patristic Catholicity: The Vincentian Canon and the Consensus Patrum in Lutheran Orthodoxy*. Munich: LIT Verlag, 2015.

Stjerna, Kirsi. *Lutheran Theology: A Grammar of Faith*. London: Bloomsbury, 2020.

Stone, Darwell. *A History of the Doctrine of the Holy Eucharist*. 1909. Reprint, Eugene, OR: Wipf & Stock, 2007.

Summers, Kirk M. *Morality After Calvin: Theodore Beza's Christian Censor and Reformed Ethics*. Oxford: Oxford University Press, 2017.

Svensson, Leif. *A Theology for the Bildungsbürgertum: Albrecht Ritschl in Context*. Berlin: de Gruyter, 2020.

Tavuzzi, Michael M. *Prierias: The Life and Works of Silvestro Mazzolini Da Prierio, 1456–1527*. Durham: Duke University Press, 1997.

Taylor, Marion A., and Agnes Choi, eds. *Handbook of Women Biblical Interpreters: A Historical and Biographical Guide*. Grand Rapids: Baker Academic, 2012.

Thomas, Andrew L. *The Apocalypse in Reformation Nuremberg: Jews and Turks in Andreas Osiander's World*. Ann Arbor: University of Michigan Press, 2022.

Bibliography

Thompson, John L. "Rules Proved by Exceptions: The Exegesis of Paul and Women in the Sixteenth Century." In *A Companion to Paul in the Reformation*, edited by R. Ward Holder, 501–40. Leiden: Brill, 2009.

Thompson, Mark D. *Celebrating the Reformation: Its Legacy and Continuing Relevance*. London: SPCK, 2017.

Thompson-Uberuaga, William. *Jesus and the Gospel Movement: Not Afraid to Be Partners*. Columbia: University of Missouri Press, 2006.

Timmerman, Daniël. *Heinrich Bullinger on Prophecy and the Prophetic Office (1523–1538)*. Göttingen: Vandenhoeck & Ruprecht, 2015.

Tipson, Baird. *Inward Baptism: The Theological Origins of Evangelicalism*. Oxford: Oxford University Press, 2020.

Toews, Abraham P. *The Problem of Mennonite Ethics*. 1963. Reprint, Eugene, OR: Wipf & Stock, 2012.

Toon, Peter. *Justification and Sanctification*. 1983. Reprint, Eugene, OR: Wipf & Stock, 2018.

Torvend, Samuel. *Luther and the Hungry Poor: Gathered Fragments*. 2008. Reprint, Eugene, OR: Wipf & Stock, 2018.

Tucker, Ruth A. *Extraordinary Women of Christian History: What We Can Learn from Their Struggles and Triumphs*. Grand Rapids: Baker, 2016.

Uhlhorn, G., and U. Rhegius. *Urbanus Rhegius: Leben Und Ausgewählte Schriften*. Elberfeld: Friedrichs, 1861.

Vainio, Olli-Pekka. *Justification and Participation in Christ: The Development of the Lutheran Doctrine of Justification from Luther to the Formula of Concord (1580)*. Studies in Medieval and Reformation Traditions 130. Leiden: Brill, 2008.

vande Kappelle, Robert P. *The New Creation: Church History Made Accessible, Relevant, and Personal*. Eugene, OR: Wipf & Stock, 2018.

Varkey, Wilson. *Role of the Holy Spirit in Protestant Systematic Theology: A Comparative Study between Karl Barth, Jürgen Moltmann, and Wolfhart Pannenberg*. London: Langham Monographs, 2011.

Vermigli, Pietro M. *Discorso Di M. Pietro Martire Vermiglii Fiorentino . . . Fatto Ne l'honoratissima Scuola Ossoniense in Inghilterra Intorno al Sacramento de l'Eucaristia*. Geneva: Burgese, Dauodeo & Iacchi, 1557.

Viazovski, Yaroslav. *Image and Hope: John Calvin and Karl Barth on Body, Soul, and Life Everlasting*. Cambridge: Lutterworth, 2016.

Vio Cajetan, Tomasso de. *Cajetan Responds: A Reader in Reformation Controversy*. Edited and translated by Jared Wicks. 1978. Reprint, Eugene, OR: Wipf & Stock, 2011.

Voak, Nigel. *Richard Hooker and Reformed Theology: A Study of Reason, Will, and Grace*. Oxford: Oxford University Press, 2003.

Voogt, Gerrit. *Constraint on Trial: Dirck Volckertsz Coornhert and Religious Freedom*. Hilversum: Verloren, 2020.

Voolstra, Sjouka. "Menno Simons." In *The Reformation Theologians: An Introduction to Theology in the Early Modern Period*, edited by Carter Lindberg, 363–77. Oxford: Wiley, 2017.

Vorster, Nico. *The Brightest Mirror of God's Works: John Calvin's Theological Anthropology*. Princeton Theological Monograph Series 236. Eugene, OR: Pickwick Publications, 2019.

Wabuda, Susan. *Thomas Cranmer*. London: Routledge, 2017.

Bibliography

Wait, Eugene M. *Great Challenges of Reformation Europe*. Huntington, NY: Nova Science, 2001.
Wallace, Ronald. *Calvin's Doctrine of The Christian Life*. 1959. Reprint, Eugene, OR: Wipf & Stock, 1997.
Waltke, Bruce K., et al. *The Psalms as Christian Worship: An Historical Commentary*. Grand Rapids: Eerdmans, 2010.
Wandel, Lee P. *The Eucharist in the Reformation*. Cambridge: Cambridge University Press, 2006.
Watson, Natalie K. *Feminist Theology*. Grand Rapids: Eerdmans, 2003.
Webb, Stephen H. *Jesus Christ, Eternal God: Heavenly Flesh and the Metaphysics of Matter*. Oxford: Oxford University Press, 2011.
Welch, Claude. *Protestant Thought in the Nineteenth Century*. Vol. 2. 1972. Reprint, Eugene, OR: Wipf & Stock, 2003.
Wengert, Timothy J. *Defending Faith: Lutheran Responses to Andreas Osiander's Doctrine of Justification, 1551–1559*. Spätmittelalter, Humanismus, Reformation 134. Tübingen: Mohr Siebeck, 2012.
———. *Human Freedom, Christian Righteousness: Philip Melanchthon's Exegetical Dispute with Erasmus of Rotterdam*. Oxford: Oxford University Press, 1998.
Westermarck, Edward. *Christianity and Morals*. New York: Macmillan, 1939.
Wheeler, Garon. *Language Teaching through the Ages*. Routledge Research in Education 93. New York: Routledge, 2013.
Wicks, Jared. *Luther's Reform: Studies on Conversion and the Church*. 1992. Reprint, Eugene, OR: Wipf & Stock, 2019.
Wiesner, Merry E. *Women and Gender in Early Modern Europe*. New Approaches to European History 41. Cambridge: Cambridge University Press, 2000.
Williams, George H. *The Radical Reformation*. Kirksville, MO: Truman State University Press, 2000.
Wilson, Derek. *Out of the Storm: The Life and Legacy of Martin Luther*. New York: St. Martin's, 2008.
Wright, Anthony D. *The Counter-Reformation: Catholic Europe and the Non-Christian World*. Rev. ed. London: Routledge, 2005.
Yarnell, Malcolm B., III. "The Person and Work of the Holy Spirit." In *A Theology for the Church*, edited by Daniel L. Akin, 483–540. Brentwood: Broadman & Holman, 2014.
Zachman, Randall C. *John Calvin as Teacher, Pastor, and Theologian: The Shape of His Writings and Thought*. Grand Rapids: Baker Academic, 2006.
Zimmermann, Jens. *Recovering Theological Hermeneutics: An Incarnational-Trinitarian Theory of Interpretation*. 2004. Reprint, Eugene, OR: Wipf & Stock, 2012.
Zorzin, Alejandro. "Andreas Bodenstein von Karlstadt." In *The Reformation Theologians: An Introduction to Theology in the Early Modern Period*, edited by Carter Lindberg, 327–37. Great Theologians. Oxford: Blackwell, 2017.
Zuidema, Jason. *Peter Martyr Vermigli (1499–1562) and the Outward Instruments of Divine Grace*. Reformed Historical Theology 4. Göttingen: Vandenhoeck & Ruprecht, 2008.
Zweig, Stefan. *Erasmus of Rotterdam*. New York: Plunkett Lake, 2019.
Zwingli, Ulrich. *Selected Works*. Translated by Samuel Macauley Jackson. 1901. Reprint, Philadelphia: University of Pennsylvania Press, 1972.

www.ingramcontent.com/pod-product-compliance
Lightning Source LLC
Chambersburg PA
CBHW022122160426
43197CB00009B/1124